The Gardener's Guide to Growing

HARDY GERANIUMS

The Gardener's Guide to Growing

HARDY GERANIUMS

Trevor Bath & Joy Jones

*Including life-size studio portraits
of many species and varieties*

TIMBER PRESS
Portland, Oregon

PAGE 2
A clump of *Geranium sanguineum* at the front of the border
has its bright flowers emphasised by the dark foliage of
Sedum 'Vera Jameson' next to it. The colour association
carries on through *Stachys macrantha* and *Knautia
macedonica* to *Clematis* 'Etoile Violette' at the back

First published 1994

Trevor Bath and Joy Jones have asserted their right to be
identified as authors of this work in accordance with the
Copyright, Designs and Patents Act 1988.

Typeset in England by ABM Typographics Ltd, Hull
and printed in Italy by New Interlitho SpA
for David & Charles
Brunel House Newton Abbot Devon

First published in North America in 1994 by
Timber Press, Inc.
9999 S.W. Wilshire, Suite 124
Portland, Oregon 97225, USA

ISBN 0–88192–278–1

CONTENTS

Introduction *by Rosemary Verey*   6

1   A Wealth of Geraniums   8

2   Geraniums in the Garden   14

3   Cultivation   53

4   Propagation   57

5   Historical and Herbal   62

6   People and Their Plants   64
    Geraniums collected in the Wild *by Roy Lancaster*
    In search of Geraniums *by Bill Baker*

7   The National Collections   78

8   Geraniums in North America   86

9   Geraniums in Australia *by Trevor Nottle*   92

10   Geraniums in New Zealand *by Malcolm Shearer*   101

11   A-Z List of Geraniums in Cultivation   102

    Appendix:

    Where to See Geraniums   147

    Where to Buy Geraniums   148

    Reading about Geraniums   150

    The Authors   151

    Acknowledgements   153

    Index   155

INTRODUCTION

This is an inspired book which I have found hard to put down, and wish it had been in my library for years. Geraniums have been growing in my garden since the renowned gardener and plant hunter, Nancy Lindsay, influenced my own first attempts at planting flower borders. She advised me, as a beginner, to grow easy plants; those with foliage and flowers to make a year-long contribution. When these had succeeded, I could branch out and use a more sophisticated palette.

After my first visit to her garden and nursery, among the euphorbias, bergenias, symphytums, hostas, bocconias and hellebores I brought home, were great clumps of hardy geraniums. All these became the backbone of my planting. Playing a major role were the geraniums G. *endressii* and G.e. 'Wargrave Pink', G. *sanguineum*, G.s. *lancastriense*, G.s. 'Glenluce', G. *pratense* and G. *phaeum*.

G. × *oxonianum* 'Claridge Druce', perpetually rosy all summer and a wonderful infiller, came later. Not a large selection, but I felt I had done well, and although this was thirty years ago they have survived, multiplied and self-sown — sometimes promiscuously — in crevices in the pathways, demanding the minimum of work. I would keep them for the beauty of their foliage alone.

Being a practical gardener, I looked to see what this book had to say about one of my favourite species. 'Of the smaller plants, G. *sanguineum* and its forms are most spectacular . . . The leaves are intricately cut . . . the addition

of autumn colouring, ranging through shades of red to gold, emphasises and dramatises the filigree effect, so they look like sprays of burning snow crystals.' Can you wonder that I cherish this plant? It is always an excitement when the leaves turn red, bronze and orange in autumn, and we hate the moment when they lose this lustre and must be tidied away. The forms of G. *endressii* keep their foliage through winter, and so does G. *phaeum* – green leaves of every shade are so welcome in winter.

I know I will turn to the chapter on 'Hardy Geraniums in the Garden' over and over again. The flowers of G. *psilostemon* are such a strong colour that I have found myself wondering what to put them with. Here there are plenty of ideas – *Berberis thunbergii atropurpurea* and *Cotinus coggygria* 'Royal Purple' with grey foliage or with *Rosa glauca*. If you want a clash, then try it with orange alstroemeria and *Lilium croceum*. There is no need ever to be dull. For 'a refreshing sorbet after a rich meal', white geraniums make a handsome contribution to a grey- and white-leaved garden. Try the double white, G. *pratense* 'Plenum Album', and G. *macrorrhizum album*.

After hearing Trevor Bath lecture, I urged him to share his knowledge and experience, of which he has more than enough to fill a volume. He has chosen to enrich this book by collaborating with Joy Jones, who runs the Hardy Geranium Group of the Hardy Plant Society, and by including articles by Roy Lancaster, Bill Baker, Dr Peter Yeo,

The bright purple-flowered *G. wallichianum* 'Syabru' was recently introduced to the UK from Nepal. It is shown here effectively draping part of the rock garden at Wisley in Surrey, contrasting with a clump of the blue-flowered form of *Parahebe catarractae*

Rosemary Lee, John Hobson and Judith Bradshaw. It is fun, and gives a wider perspective, to read the articles on geraniums in Australia, New Zealand and North America. To complete the pleasure, Trevor and Joy list nurseries and gardens where geraniums can be seen growing.

I guarantee that after this book is published there will be an upsurge in demand for hardy geraniums, as more and more people discover, as I have done, their versatility. There are nearly 230 varieties described in the book, and no doubt many more waiting in the wings. Who will create the first all-geranium garden, maybe with bulbs piercing through them?

ROSEMARY VEREY
Barnsley House,
Gloucestershire

1
A WEALTH
OF GERANIUMS

Gradually, inevitably, geraniums have been emerging from the shadows into the spotlight in recent years. At one time they had a very low profile, and were considered only as fillers, or bread-and-butter plants. One of their qualities is being good-natured, and they seemed quite content with a supporting role, but then it became increasingly apparent that they were rising stars with great potential. New species were introduced, new hybrids created, and at last they began to get the media coverage which sets the fashion in plants, as in so many other things – although in this case it is a fashion which is far from fleeting. Their new prominence only served to highlight their many excellent garden qualities, their versatility and their durability.

Most good gardens today feature an increasing variety of geraniums, used in a number of different ways. On an everyday level they will put up with being stuck in anywhere to fill a gap and still come up smiling, with a long display of flowers and an even more extended show of attractive foliage. But they deserve much better than that. A little attention paid to their cultural preferences, and the very many ways in which they can be shown to advantage in the garden, will be greatly rewarded. You can use them in large groups of the same variety, or mix and match them in more individual and subtle associations with other plants of all kinds. Their array of flower colour and diversity of leaf shape, in both cases running the gamut from delicate to robust, offers tremendous scope.

There are geraniums in a series of heights from 4in (10cm) to 48in (122cm), so they will fit into any situation, from an alpine trough to a wild woodland setting. Their ease of cultivation and maintenance makes them ideal for today's gardens, where the main requirement is for a pleasing, long-term effect which does not need a great deal of upkeep. At the same time, among the wide choice of geraniums introduced, there are also some unusual varieties of limited availability which have great appeal for the collector.

There is, of course, the little matter of the confusion between geraniums and pelargoniums. Some people prefer to treat it as a joke, on the lines of, 'When is a geranium not a geranium?' 'When it's a pelargonium', shrugging it off as a merry mix-up. The maddening muddle goes back to the eighteenth century, when Linnaeus (Carl von Linné), the father of modern taxonomy, introduced the binomial system for the naming of plants. Each plant was given two Latin names, a generic name referring to its family, and a specific name referring to itself. In 1738 it had been proposed that pelargoniums and geraniums should be distinct groups, but for some reason Linnaeus would not accept this, and lumped them together under the general heading of 'Geraniums'. This name soon became one which was commonly supposed to refer *only* to pelargoniums, which increased in popularity when a number of new species were introduced from South Africa and

This eye-catching selection of pinks and purples includes *G. psilostemon*, *G.p.* 'Bressingham Flair', *G. sanguineum* var. *striatum* and assorted forms of *G.* × *oxonianum* (Plant material from Trevor Bath's garden)

10

became the mainstay of Victorian and Edwardian bedding-out schemes.

At that time very few of the true geraniums were available, or widely grown, while the usurping pelargoniums went from strength to strength. Today the vast majority of people still refer to pelargoniums as 'geraniums'. As Hugh Johnson says in *The Principles of Gardening* (1979), 'It is one of the rare cases in horticulture where democracy has successfully routed botany'. Books with 'Geranium' in their titles are usually found to refer only to pelargoniums. At least two specialist 'geranium' nurseries in the UK deal exclusively in pelargoniums.

It is hardly surprising then that my early childhood memories of pot-plants on the kitchen window-sill should be dominated by the bright scarlet flowers of the 'geraniums'. Among the profusion of wild flowers in the hedges and fields around that Dorset village, the only remembered wild geranium is G. *robertianum*, always known as 'Herb Robert' and taken for granted with its simple charm. School fêtes and other summer festivities were held in the grounds of the rectory, where the borders featured clumps of glorious blue flowers, identified much later as G. × *magnificum*.

In later years, living in London and joining the Royal Horticultural Society meant regular visits to the flower shows which were then held every fortnight at Vincent Square. My long-term membership of the Hardy Plant Society (HPS) resulted from seeing one of their attractive displays there. Margery Fish was one of the founder members of the HPS, and her first book, *We Made a Garden* (1956) made a great impression on me, with the matter-of-fact warmth and wisdom of her style. She wrote about many of the traditional plants I remembered from my childhood – at last I could give them a name. Not many geraniums are mentioned in that first

The strikingly rich colours of *Geranium* x *magnificum* and G. *psilostemon*, and the lighter tones of G. 'Johnson's Blue' are highlighted by the bright leaves of *Spiraea* 'Gold Flame' and the yellow-green heads of *Euphorbia characias* ssp. *wulfenii*, with a dark mat of *Ajuga reptans* 'Atropurpurea' as a footnote

book, but enough to whet my appetite – an appetite which was inflamed by my first visit to her garden at East Lambrook, with its revelatory planting.

I paid many visits to East Lambrook Manor while Margery Fish was still alive, and through meeting her, corresponding with her and buying plants from her, my attraction to geraniums was greatly fostered. One of my most treasured plants is a G. *psilostemon* which came from her; it survived for years in a tiny London back garden before being transferred to the garden of my present home in Surrey, where I found a fellow enthusiast living nearby. This was Joy Forty (now Joy Jones), another member of the HPS, who was already an expert on geraniums, and very generous in sharing her collection of plants and her knowledge.

When I established a nursery called 'Plants for Pleasure' it specialised in cottage garden plants, a rather loose definition but including an increasing number of geraniums. Among the plants that I raised and introduced was an improved form of G. *phaeum*, named G.p. 'Lily Lovell' after my mother. This has good foliage, a paler green than the type, contrasting well with the large, deep mauve flowers with their paler centres. Anyhow, that's how I described it, but reaction to colour is very personal.

FLOWER COLOUR

The use of the Royal Horticultural Society's Colour Chart does not seem absolutely conclusive, even if it were less expensive and less complex to use for the ordinary gardener. In many geranium flowers the basic colour is overlaid with many delicate graduations and shadings. The report on the Wisley Trial of geraniums in 1976 quotes the flower colour of G. 'Johnson's Blue' as 'Violet Blue Group 94B tinged with Violet Blue Group 94A, flushed towards the base of petal with Purple Group 77A'!

In everyday practice so much depends on the eye of the beholder and the individual interpretation of such ambiguous words as 'mauve' and 'purple'. There is also the fact that plants grown under different conditions and in different situations may well vary from the accepted norm.

Good blue flowers are often in short supply in the summer garden, but geraniums go a long way towards filling this need, though admittedly quite a few of them veer towards violet tones. The recently introduced hybrid G. 'Brookside' is one of the truest blues, followed later in the season by the paler G. *wallichianum* 'Buxton's Variety'. Many geraniums come in varying degrees of pink, of which my personal favourite is the clear colour of G. *clarkei* 'Kashmir Pink'. There are also a few rich and resounding purples, such as G. *psilostemon*, G. *cinereum* var. *subcaulescens* and G. *wallichianum* 'Syabru'. At the other end of the scale are some most attractive white forms, which between them span the main flowering season and cover the range of options from dead-white to off-white, sometimes warmed with a pink flush or veining.

FOLIAGE

Less attention is usually given to geranium foliage, a grave omission as it contributes a very positive element to the garden scene. It was leaves that brought many of the geraniums to public notice in the first place. Their miscellany of shapes and textures, and their long-lasting qualities make them an obvious choice for reliable and ornamental ground cover. From there, it was only a matter of time before their true worth as all-round garden plants was recognised, and this growing awareness brought about an increasing supply of even more attractive garden varieties.

This in turn has brought about a situation where there may be a temptation for newly introduced species and newly developed hybrids to be brought on to the market before their potential has been fully investigated. Because of the ease with which many species hybridise naturally, any gardener or nurseryman who grows a representative selection will soon find a few seedlings of mixed blood popping up. The acid test is to determine whether a new seedling is sufficiently different from its parents, or any other existing varieties, to embark on a career of its own. Will it retain whatever special characteristics attracted attention to it in the first place? Will it prove garden-worthy when grown under trial conditions for an extensive period, or will it prove to be just a flash in the seed pan?

In this book we have tried to describe as many as possible of the geranium species and varieties currently available, together with suggestions on how to use them effectively in different garden situations. To reduce the confusion about the generic name it is now becoming quite a usual practice to refer to hardy geraniums as 'cultivated cranesbills'. This seems an admirable compromise, combining a reference to their wild origin and the degree to which they are now being welcomed into gardens.

It may be a form of mild insanity to suppose that certain plants are invested with human sensibilities, but these cultivated cranesbills do seem to exude a calm benevolence, an air of being comfortably at ease in their surroundings — characteristics which helped to establish their attraction for me in the first place.

2

GERANIUMS
IN THE GARDEN

Geraniums are, in the main, extremely adaptable and tolerant garden plants, with varieties suitable for almost every site and situation. In this chapter we look at some of the ways in which they can be used, and suggest groupings and companion plants to create pleasing associations in beds, borders and containers.

MIXED PLANTING

Mixed planting is a very variable style which can be adapted for any area. It means that there is a much greater flexibility for accommodating all sorts of plants, and combining them to provide a changing pattern of interest over a long season. Shrubs are the key to which all the other notes – perennials, biennials, annuals and bulbs – can be related. There is a very wide choice of shrubs, but those with distinctive foliage, which are not only attractive in themselves but will also create a congenial setting for the other plants, are the most rewarding. Geraniums associate particularly well with shrubs because of their varying heights, extended flowering periods and the diverse sizes and textures of their long-lasting leaves.

BOLD GROUPING

Nervous gardeners have been known to fight shy of *Geranium psilostemon* because they feel it might be difficult to place. This is a pity, as it is an excellent perennial and can be used in many combinations of mixed plants. It is one of the tallest and most striking geraniums at around 36-48in (91-122cm) and has large, rounded flowers in brilliant magenta with dramatic black eyes and veining. It associates well with purple-leaved shrubs such as *Berberis thunbergii* forma *atropurpurea* and *Cotinus coggygria* 'Royal Purple', both of which will add their autumn colour to that of the geranium leaves. *G. psilostemon* also looks very distinguished with silver or grey-leaved shrubs such as the weeping silver pear (*Pyrus salicifolia* 'Pendula'), sea buckthorn (*Rhamnus alaternus*) or *Buddleia alternifolia* 'Argentea'.

The species rose *Rosa glauca* (formerly *R. rubrifolia*) has the best of both worlds as its pewter-grey leaves are overlaid with a purple flush, providing a subtle foil for *G. psilostemon*. The rose benefits from being cut back drastically every few years, which will encourage fresh young growth with much larger and brighter leaves.

Whichever shrubs are chosen to partner *Geranium psilostemon*, either purple or grey, they can be underplanted with *Artemisia ludoviciana*, with its narrow silver leaves on upright stems, and the airy filigree of *A.* 'Powis Castle' to provide a cool metallic undertone. This can be contrasted in turn with the ecclesiastical purple of the annual *Atriplex hortensis* 'Rubra'. A subdued echo of the geranium could be included in the shape of its offspring *G.p.* 'Bressingham Flair', a shorter form with less intense colour and so less personality.

This magnificent specimen of G. *psilostemon* is cleverly balanced by the contrasting texture, colour and sheer volume of the weeping pear. The detailed underplanting of the geranium includes *Allium albopilosum* and *Santolina neapolitana* 'Edward Bowles'

16

For a different type of grouping there are many possibilities in the 'dramatic clash' school of thought. Walter Ingwersen suggested 'rich orange-coloured neighbours' to go with G. *psilostemon*, and Graham Stuart Thomas carries this a stage further by specifying orange alstroemerias and *Lilium croceum*. Christopher Lloyd, a noted clasher, suggests purple and yellow for a colour scheme.

Certainly I have found that the lemon-yellow anthemis *A. tinctoria* 'E.C. Buxton' looks very good with G. *psilostemon*, as well as being one of the longest-flowering plants in the border. The tall spires of *Verbascum bombyciferum* give a useful change of height and shape. They also furnish handsome rosettes of silver leaves throughout the previous winter. *V.* 'Gainsborough' has masses of soft yellow flowers on shorter, many-branched stems, but is a somewhat short-lived perennial, unlike *Potentilla recta* 'Citrina' (*P.r. pallida*) which is thoroughly reliable. Its delicately yellow flowers, like pale buttercups, are

Geranium psilostemon and *Campanula latifolia* 'Brantwood' make a richly coloured partnership, sharpened with an underplanting of *Alchemilla mollis*

The brilliantly coloured flowers of *Geranium* × *riversleaianum* 'Russell Prichard' are well matched by its companions in the border, including *Scabiosa* 'Butterfly Blue' and *Penstemon* 'Rich Ruby'

displayed all summer above dark green digitate leaves, and seedlings come true.

The flowers of G. *psilostemon* may be a strong colour but it is a clear one, and can therefore be teamed with other flowers having equally rich but pure colours, giving the sort of effect produced in stained glass. Try it with a good clump of *Campanula latifolia* 'Brantwood' for a satisfying partnership, with just a touch of acid-yellow from *Alchemilla mollis* to intensify the richness still further. I have also seen a superb mass planting at Lawhead Croft in Scotland in bright pinks and purples, consisting of G. *psilostemon* with *Mimulus lewisii* and *Lychnis flos-jovis*.

Two other tall geraniums that look well with red- or silver-leaved shrubs are *Geranium × oxonianum* 'Thurstonianum' and *G. × o.* 'Lady Moore', both around 24-36in (61-91cm). The former has a very long succession of flowers with curiously narrow, blunt petals set widely apart. Individually the flowers may look under-developed, but there is always such a lavish display of them in jewel-like purple from mid-summer to the frosts that the overall impression is very pleasing. As an additional feature, many of the flowers at the beginning of the season are semi-double, having produced petaloid stamens as well as petals.

Geranium × o. 'Lady Moore' is a good plant with an enigmatic history. It was mentioned by Margery Fish in her book *Gardening in the Shade* as having been given to her by Lady Moore, the only information about its provenance being that it had been given to *her* by a clergyman with a black beard. Lady Moore was the wife of Sir Frederick Moore, director of the Dublin Botanic Gardens for many years, but she was also a considerable gardener and plantswoman in her own right. Her namesake plant has large open flowers, clear pinky-purple with darker veins, and a long flowering season. Both it and *G. × o.* 'Thurstonianum' make large billowing clumps and do need some support. This could be given to them by shrubs, through which they could intertwine.

A PALE SURPRISE

I remember going to Lord King's garden at Wartnaby in Leicestershire some years ago. It was high summer, and the main part of the garden was overflowing with old roses and excellent perennials in full flower. But when I came across a small enclosure planted in white and silver, with the damask rose 'Madame Hardy', *Eleagnus commutata*, white valerian (*Centranthus ruber*

At East Lambrook Manor, this pale and subtle planting contrasts the styles and textures of *Geranium macrorrhizum* 'Album' and *G. sylvaticum* 'Album', nicely pointed up by a good silvery-leaved form of *Pulmonaria saccharata*

'Albus') and white delphiniums, it was like a refreshing sorbet after a rich meal. Every garden needs an unexpected area with a different style of planting to give it that element of surprise and interest, and a colour grouping in white or soft pastel shades is one way to achieve this. For the best effect, a planting of this sort should be enclosed, and slightly apart from the main garden. It is also a good way to cheer up a nondescript area or a neglected corner.

To extend the interest, the white or pale flowers should be backed up not only with silver and grey foliage, but also by the interplay of leaves in every shade of green. This was very much in the mind of Vita Sackville-West when she wrote about her 'grey, green and white' garden at Sissinghurst Castle in Kent. There seems to be no evidence that she herself ever referred to it as 'The White Garden', by which title it is now known worldwide. It remains a classic example of how to use foliage in subtle and varied ways to enhance and offset the flowers, and to many visitors it is still, over forty years after its creation, the heart and soul of Sissinghurst. It is full of ideas which can be used in much more modest groupings and 'incidents'. The many white-flowered forms of geraniums are ideal for this, with their extended flowering periods and wide array of leaf shapes.

My first choice of geranium to use in a white planting would be the double white *Geranium pratense* 'Plenum Album'. It is not often seen, and is rather a shy plant, but could be made into a star feature with the right siting and associations. The flowers are loosely petalled, with a pale mauve centre which gives an opportunity to strike a responsive chord in other plants, such as *Verbascum chaixii* 'Album'. This verbascum is a sturdy plant with a basal rosette of large dark green leaves, and flower spikes up to 36in (91cm). Each stem is completely covered with small, creamy-white flowers featuring purple stamens and orange anthers. An even stronger accompaniment would be *Acanthus spinosus*, its white flowers hooded with purple bracts borne on stout stems above a dramatic spread of architectural leaves. The softer, broader leaves

20

of *Acanthus mollis*, with flowers similar to *A. spinosus*, could be used as an alternative. These suggested groupings could of course be integrated into a larger scheme, but might also be used as white incidents to highlight a mixed border.

At the front of the group, the soft greyish leaves of *Geranium renardii* could be offset by the permanent silver-blue leaves of a white-flowered dianthus, such as the old favourite *Dianthus* 'Mrs Sinkins' or the more refined single, green-eyed *D.* 'Musgrave's Pink'. To contrast with these, the sea urchin mounds of *Festuca glauca*, the blue fescue grass, and the silver heart-shaped leaves of *Lamium maculatum* 'White Nancy' could be used. For added height, try *Cnicus benedictus*, the Blessed Thistle, which rises up to 24in (61cm) from a rosette of narrow, spiny leaves with wonderful silver-variegated patterns.

For the ideal edging, try a white-flowered form of *Geranium endressii*. I found a good one in a batch of seedlings and, having grown it on for some years, find that the colour is consistent and the flowers only take on a pinkish tinge in their last stages. The white-flowered form of *G. maculatum* would look crisp and cool whatever the weather. In late spring, *G. sylvaticum album* would put on an arresting mass display of upward-looking flowers with palest green centres. This plant is particularly effective when allowed to grow into a large clump.

In early summer, *Geranium pratense* forma *albiflorum* would take over, with its larger, flatter flowers. This is another good choice for a large group and would look well under a flowering shrub such as *Rosa rugosa* 'Blanc Double de Coubert', *Hoheria sexstylosa* or a philadelphus, with the tall, spiked heads of *Veronica virginica alba* rising to one side, and a white astilbe in

A double planting of *Geranium endressii* is easily assimilated into a border which also contains a bright red *Hedysarum coronarium*, leading the eye to *Clematis* 'Rouge Cardinal' on the wall, while low mats of *Geranium* x *oxonianum* 'Winscombe', *Lamium maculatum roseum* and *G. macrorrhizum* complete the grouping

22

front. Flanking these, a white-flowered hosta would fit in well. The choice is between a glaucous-leaved variety such as *Hosta sieboldiana elegans* or a green-leaved form like *H. sieboldii alba*. Trailing through all these and forming a visual link, a white-flowered form of *Geranium asphodeloides* would be attractive. The hybrid *G.a.* 'Starlight', in which the petals are broader and denser, would make a more solid effect.

There is another form of *Geranium pratense*, *G.p.* 'Silver Queen' which is less prolific and more ethereal. The flowers are a strange off-white, almost grey, with prominent dark veining and stamens. A particularly subtle companion for grey foliage, this is another name which is often misapplied, even to plants with bright blue flowers! The true plant would make a felicitous combination with *Eleagnus ebbingei*, under-planted with the blue grass *Agropyron glaucum*, the papery white flowers and woolly leaves of *Anaphalis triplinervis* and a sprinkling of annual poppies in the selected 'Mother-of-Pearl' strain with its predominance of grey, pale blue and white shades. Any pale pink poppies could be rooted out, or left in to strike a different note against the predominantly grey, green and white planting. This could be echoed by white flowers with an intriguing touch of pink, such as *Geranium clarkei* 'Kashmir White', *Centaurea montana carnea* and *Malva moschata* 'Alba', with its central pink stamens accentuating the purity of the white flowers against the dark green leaves.

DOUBLE DELIGHTS

The double-flowered forms of *Geranium pratense* are always excellent value in mixed plantings. *G.p.* 'Plenum Caeruleum' has informally shaped, double flowers in a soft, almost faded

Geranium x *magnificum* is the centrepiece of a dazzling summer display. Contrast in height, texture and colour is provided by the feathery plumes of *Aruncus dioicus* and a planting of the gold-striped grass *Hakonechloa macra* 'Albo-aurea' in a terracotta container. Foreground interest is supplied by *Geranium endressii*, *Geranium asphodeloides* and *Alchemilla mollis*

mauvey-blue with a rosy centre, carried in quantity on tall stems. Alice Coats, the garden historian and artist, compared their 'charming little flowers' to Parma violets in her book *Flowers and Their Histories*. Unfortunately the analogy is incomplete, as they are not scented.

All double geraniums are sterile and so are notably long flowering, not needing to waste time or energy on seed production. The double blue in particular has an aristocratic look, an air of having known a gentler world, but is still prepared to smile graciously on its present surroundings, giving a traditional and historic effect – an old-world charm – to any garden where it is grown, fitting in exceptionally well in the gardens of stately homes and National Trust properties.

There is an outstanding garden at Chilcombe in Dorset, created by an American artist, John Hubbard and his wife Caryl. The artistic touch is very evident in the many restful plant associations, often using soft blues and mauves. The double blue geranium is skilfully employed in several places, most notably in association with lavender, nearly matched by the delicate blue of *Polemonium caeruleum* ('Jacob's Ladder'), *Viola cornuta* in both white and lilac, and the more definite shape and colour of *Erigeron* 'Darkest of All'. Other possible companions include the papery lavender-blue flowers of *Catananche caerulea* ('Cupid's Dart') and *Salvia sclarea* var. *turkestanica* with its pink-lilac bracts and flowers. This salvia also has a strong, clinging scent, politely called 'pineapple' but in my opinion much more like body odour.

The double violet geranium, *G.p.* 'Plenum Violaceum' (quite often referred to as double purple) has flowers in a more symmetrical rosette and a stronger, deeper colour – a rich mauve-purple with a stronger purple shading at the base of the petals, changing to a pale greeny-yellow right at the centre. A compatible colour comes from *Campanula latiloba* 'Highcliffe' with large starry flowers pressed closely against the 36in (91cm) stems. These two plants would gain greatly from the addition of *Verbascum chaixii* with its clear yellow flowers with a purple

eye and dark green leaves, giving just the right astringent touch. Other possibilities include *Monarda* 'Beauty of Cobham' with its pale pink flowers and deeper coloured bracts, the dark purple *Monarda* 'Prairie Night', *Aster* × *frikartii* 'Mönch' and the purple- or bronze-leafed fennel.

A TOUCH OF THE BLUES

A geranium with a remarkably long flowering season, due to its being a sterile hybrid, is *Geranium* 'Johnson's Blue'. It has great charm and elegance, with finely cut leaves enhancing the flat, open flowers which have pointed petals of a clear mid-blue and a paler centre, giving an almost luminous effect. The delicate foliage would be shown off well by the glossily solid green leaves of bergenias and the rich purple leaves of *Heuchera micrantha* 'Palace Purple', with a foreground planting of *Ajuga reptans* 'Atropurpurea'. The distinctive colour of the flowers would be pointed up by the pale yellow rock rose, *Helianthemum* 'Wisley Primrose' and, later on, pale pink penstemons such as P. 'Hidcote Pink' or P. 'Evelyn'. A clump of *Camassia leichtlinii* with spikes of dark blue star flowers would add dramatic interest to the group.

It is unfortunate that wrongly labelled geraniums are often supplied by nurseries and garden centres instead of the correct variety. Many plants which their owners fondly imagine to be the real *Geranium* 'Johnson's Blue' turn out to be G. × *magnificum*, G. *ibericum*, G. *platypetalum* or G. *himalayense*. These are all good plants in their own right, but are not in the same class for distinction and long-flowering as the real thing.

Geranium himalayense fits in anywhere and also extends over a long season. It makes a low, compact plant (or 'tuffet' to quote Graham Stuart Thomas) with large, round flowers of deep mauve-blue. It is often associated with yellow roses, but a more practical companion for a small garden would be one of the shrubby potentillas with pale yellow flowers, such as *Potentilla* 'Primrose Beauty' or the even paler P. 'Tilford Cream'. The deep velvety-red viola with a black blotch, *Viola* 'Arkwright's Ruby' would pick up the red colouration in the centre of the geranium flower, with the pale yellow *Achillea* 'Moonshine' to echo the potentilla, and the narrow spikes of *Salvia* × *superba* striking a richer note. As a further attraction, the reddish bracts of the salvia are retained on the stems after the flowers have dropped.

The variety *Geranium himalayense* 'Gravetye' is a slightly smaller plant but with bigger flowers which have a more pronounced reddish marking in the centre. It increases gradually by underground rhizomes but is not invasive. An even more desirable form is *G.h.* 'Irish Blue', discovered by Graham Stuart Thomas in an Irish garden. The large flowers, rather flatter than the type, are in a charming shade of light blue, with reddish backs to the petals. A flattering accompaniment would be simple flowers in cream or white, such as *Epilobium glabellum*, *Oenothera speciosa* or *Sidalcea candida*, contrasted with *Sedum* 'Ruby Glow' which has grey leaves on sprawling stems, and produces deep purple flowers later on.

One of the longest established geraniums, and a very easy-going one, is *Geranium* × *magnificum*. The leaves are quite large, dark green and coarsely textured, lasting from spring until autumn, when they take on bright colours of pink and yellow. The flowers put on a concentrated display in early summer with a spectacular succession of large violet-blue flowers, flat and well veined. Just as you've got used to seeing them every day, their season comes to an end, but the leaves go on giving excellent value as a backdrop for later-flowering plants, or as a solid foreground for such summer bulbs as *Galtonia candicans* and *Gladiolus byzantinus*. Floppy plants like *Aster divaricatus* (*A. corymbosus*) look good trailing over the geranium leaves, as do the starry flowers of *Geranium asphodeloides*. The cucumber-cool leaves of *Sedum* 'Autumn Joy' would be a striking contrast, the flat heads of pink flowers being produced to coincide with the autumn colours of the geranium foliage.

Geranium × *magnificum* is a sterile hybrid between *G. ibericum* and *G. platypetalum*, either name often being misapplied to *G.* × *magnificum*. Both the parents are superficially similar, making taller, less compact plants, their flowers being smaller, cup-shaped and of a more intense blue.

SOME INDIVIDUALS

Two distinctive forms of *Geranium pratense* which look particularly good in the border are *G.p.* 'Striatum' with flowers in random mixtures of blue and white, and *G.p.* 'Mrs Kendall Clark', an attractive plant but a lady of mystery. Apparently she was a friend of Walter Ingwersen and gave him a geranium which he introduced in the 1930s, named after her and mentioned in his booklet *The Genus Geranium* (1946). He said that the colour of the flowers was difficult to describe but 'the nearest we can get to it is pearl-grey flushed with softest rose, a colour seen in some opals or certain kinds of mother-of-pearl'. However the *G.p.* 'Mrs Kendall Clark' submitted to the Wisley trial of geraniums in 1973 by Blooms Nurseries and Mr S. M. Gault, and given an Award of Merit in 1976, was described in the Proceedings of the Royal Horticultural Society

The pale lavender, white-veined flowers of *G. pratense* 'Mrs Kendall Clark' are very distinctive, but there are doubts as to whether it is correctly named. See above and page 26 for details of the controversy

26

as 'violet blue with white veining'. This certainly matches up with the plant now widely available under that name, which has large, flat, mid-blue flowers with raised white veins which become more prominent as the flower matures. The veins converge in a way which recalls the pointed arches of Gothic architecture and the delicate tracery of church windows.

Axletree Nursery has a plant, said to be the original 'Mrs Kendall Clark', the colour of which certainly tallies with Walter Ingwersen's description. It is quite a small, cupped flower, very attractive in its way, but in my opinion nothing like as distinctive as the Award of Merit plant, which continues to be one of my favourites.

A border phlox, P. paniculata 'Prospero', would match the combination of colours in the blue and white form of Geranium pratense 'Mrs Kendall Clark' but unfortunately its season is just that little bit later. There is always the possibility with planned colour associations that the flowering times may not coincide. However, a long-flowering annual which would blend with the geranium and overlap with it is Phacelia tanacetifolia. Its scrolled flower heads have many violet-blue buds opening to pale lavender flowers, with long violet stamens giving a rather furry appearance.

Geranium pratense 'Striatum' is engagingly eccentric, its basically white flowers having individual streaks, splashes, dots and spots of blue. Sometimes four of the petals are plain white or blue, with the remaining petal in the other colour, so that every day there is the fun of going out to see the latest permutation. Fairly plain flowers are best as neighbours, so as not to detract too much from the floral fireworks of the geranium. White Campanula persicifolia in single or double forms, Malva moschata in its pale pink wild form, or its pure white garden variety M.m. alba, enhanced by pink stamens, plus the silver foliage of Artemisia ludoviciana or A. absinthium 'Lambrook Silver' set the geranium off well.

Another special plant which always attracts attention is Geranium maculatum. It was not commercially available for some time and there was also confusion about its name. Since 'maculatum' means 'spotted' it was reasonably assumed that the leaves would be prominently marked, and what you got as G. maculatum was in fact G. punctatum (of gardens) which does have a very prominent spot on each lobe. But once you've seen the real plant there is no mistaking it. A North American native of cool elegance, its pale mauve flowers are strikingly intensified by the dark stems and sparse but crisply cut leaves. The mystery remains as to why it was given its specific name, as the foliage is not noticeably spotted. Providing the soil is not too dry, G. maculatum makes a splendid planting with Thalictrum delavayi, Linaria purpurea 'Canon Went' and Campanula latiloba 'Hidcote Amethyst'.

AROUND THE SHRUBS

Shrubs which are mainly grown for the sake of their spring flowers can continue to contribute to the garden scene in summer by acting as a background to low and medium growing geraniums planted around and between them. Forsythia, ribes and Lonicera × purpusii, which are rather lacking in appeal after their flowers have faded, would benefit by being framed with groups of Geranium endressii, G. × oxonianum hybrids and G. himalayense, which will provide a different kind of interest for a further period. The more solid and sombre textures of rhododendrons and mahonias can also be lightened in this way.

Shrubs which bloom in the summer can have geraniums flowering around them at the same time, which will augment their attraction while extending the colour and interest of the area still longer. I've seen a very attractive partnership of this kind at the Hollies Park in Leeds, home of the National Collection of Philadelphus. P. 'Innocence' was underplanted with Geranium

Geranium sanguineum 'Album' makes an ideal underplanting for shrubs. Here the dead-white flowers and dark green leaves are a delicate foil for the creamy-white scented flowers and discreetly variegated leaves of Philadelphus 'Innocence'

The recently introduced hybrid G. 'Nimbus' has very delicately fretted leaves, overcast with gold, a suitably ethereal background for the large starry flowers

sanguineum 'Album', its dark green leaves and pure white flowers setting off the discreetly variegated leaves and creamy, scented flowers of the shrub. The geranium was also growing up into the lower branches of the philadelphus, which emphasised the affinity even more.

The purple-leaved weigela, W. florida 'Foliis Purpureis' can look rather dark and lowering when out of flower, but can be lightened by a low mat of Geranium sanguineum var. striatum, with the purple spikes of Gladiolus byzantinus rising through it.

GOLDEN-LEAVED SHRUBS

Golden-leaved shrubs are great favourites of mine: they give a lift to any mixed planting and look cheerful even on a dull day. I do find with the golden form of philadelphus, P. coronarius

'Aureus', that the glory of the leaves tends to eclipse the quite small flowers, so use an underplanting in a definite contrasting colour. Blue geraniums such as Geranium 'Johnson's Blue' or G. himalayense 'Gravetye' give a good effect, with sky-blue Anemone blanda using the same ground for an earlier show.

Physocarpus opulifolius 'Dart's Gold' and Choisya ternata 'Sundance' are other good examples of shrubs with sunshine leaves. The taller blue geraniums look well against these – forms of Geranium pratense selected for their good colours, or G. phaeum 'Lily Lovell' with superior dark blue flowers and pale green leaves. For a more definite outline and a change of style, try adding Phaiophleps nigricans (an uninspiring change of name for the old favourite Sisyrinchium striatum) and Kniphofia 'Little Maid'.

Berberis thunbergii 'Aurea' is a dainty golden shrub which prefers a semi-shaded spot, otherwise it may risk scorching. This can act as a host to the trailing stems of Geranium wallichianum

'Buxton's Variety' whose true-blue, white-centred, saucer-shaped flowers look even more striking against the bright leaves. This geranium also enjoys the chance of using the rigid framework of *Cotoneaster horizontalis* as a kind of climbing frame, the leaves of both taking on red tones in autumn.

A new variety of geranium called *Geranium* 'Nimbus' is another good partner for a gold shrub, as the very finely fretted leaves have a matching gold tinge when young. The large flowers are a purplish-pink with darker veins, the petals held slightly apart to give a particularly showy appearance. Its rather lax habit means that the flowering stems cover a good area, and they intermingle happily with shrubs and other upright plants. This geranium looks splendid with the gold variegated cornus, C. *alba* 'Spaethii' or, on a lower level, *Rubus parviflorus* 'Sunshine Spreader' which covers the ground without suckering, and was used to great effect as a mass planting at the Ebbw Vale Garden Festival in 1992.

TRAILING GERANIUMS

Geraniums that weave long flowering stems through the surrounding vegetation are very useful for brightening up shrubs with plain leaves, such as hypericums, which have flowered earlier. *Geranium procurrens* can be invasive when grown on the flat, as it roots at every node, forming new plants and colonising the ground at a great rate. A good way to curb this tendency, while capitalising on its rate of growth, is to plant it at the base of a fairly open shrub into which it can then climb, producing a long parade of pinkish-purple flowers with dark centres and black veins peering out amongst the shrub's leaves. It shows up well against the plain, dark green hypericum leaves, with even greater autumn interest if the shrub is one which produces coloured fruits, such as *Hypericum* × *inodorum* 'Elstead'.

Another way of keeping *Geranium procurrens* off the ground is to grow it over a low, compact shrub, preferably one which keeps its leaves all year. An ideal candidate for this sort of scheme is a shrub which has suffered a series of name changes at the hands of the taxonomists. It was originally classified as a senecio and was known variously as *S. greyi*, *S. laxifolius* and *S.* 'Dunedin Sunshine'. It has now been burdened with the name of *Brachyglottis* 'Sunshine'. It is such a remarkably adaptable plant, so good-tempered and easy-going, that it is often taken for granted. The weather-resistant leaves of soft grey make it indispensable for foliage effect throughout the year, whether used in the garden or transferred indoors for a flower arrangement. It responds well to hard pruning, which will keep a fresh supply of young shoots coming. The only disadvantage (apart from having to keep up with the new names!) is that the bright yellow daisy flowers are incompatible with practically everything and need to be removed quickly. However, in the bud stage, covered in a silvery-white down, they are most appealing, and essential for flower arrangements.

There are two attractive hybrids of *Geranium procurrens* which also throw out long arms, but without rooting down. These gain a new dimension from being supported by an obliging shrub such as brachyglottis or a shrubby potentilla. G. 'Ann Folkard' is the result of an alliance between *G. procurrens* and *G. psilostemon*. It is quite spectacular, with primrose-yellow splashes on the young leaves, and flowers which come in two shades. The new ones are in a bright colour similar to *G. psilostemon*, then change as they age to a deeper, more subdued purple. The combination of leaves and flowers is quite eye-catching and unusual, particularly as it continues flowering into the autumn. This is another geranium with an affinity with gold-leaved shrubs. At the Royal Horticultural Society's garden at Wisley in Surrey, G. 'Ann Folkard' has been used effectively as a planting around a large clump of *Sedum* 'Autumn Joy'. The sedum's solidity and rusty-red seedheads act as a visual and physical anchor for the swirling geranium.

Geranium 'Salome' is a hybrid between *G. procurrens* and *G. lambertii*. The flowers are similar in type to the former, but are larger, paler, and more dramatically veined, held in the

G. sanguineum var. *striatum* (formerly *G.s. lancastriense*) grows into a very attractive mound of dark green leaves, spangled with pale pink flowers

vertical mode of G. *lambertii*. The young leaves are characterised by the same yellowish centre as G. 'Ann Folkard'. All three geraniums – G. *procurrens*, G. 'Salome' and G. 'Ann Folkard' – are well grown and shown to advantage over low bushes of *Brachyglottis* 'Sunshine' at The Garden House, Buckland Monachorum, in Devon.

There are other low, but deciduous shrubs for foreground planting, such as the dwarf forms of purple berberis, *B. thunbergii* 'Atropurpurea Nana' and *B.t.* 'Bagatelle'. These would make striking hosts for *Geranium asphodeloides*, another weaver that sends out long trailing stems from a central crown. It has non-stop flowers in an open starry shape, variously purple, pink or white, all of which have contrasting darker veins.

There are a number of herbaceous plants with strong foliage but an early-flowering habit, such as irises and paeonies, which could be used to vary the background for these low trailing geraniums.

GERANIUMS FOR THE FRONT ROW

At the front of the planting, low mat-forming geraniums provide long-lasting interest, particularly *Geranium sanguineum* and its various forms. *G.s.* var. *striatum* is the most immediately appealing. Its palest pink flowers with deeper pink veining show up well against the dark green leaves. It is a pity that its previous name, *G.s. lancastriense*, has been changed, as it was so well-established, and referred to the plant's native habitat on Walney Island, off the coast of Lancashire. Not only has the name of the geranium been changed but also its geographical location, as bureaucracy has now ceded Walney Island to Cumbria. The flower colour of G. *sanguineum* var. *striatum* can vary quite a lot in intensity. Geoffrey Smith, in the book of his television series *The World of Flowers*, relates how he once spent a day on Walney Island trying to establish the true colour of the type. After identifying fourteen shades he gave up.

Another native variation was discovered by A. T. Johnson at Glenluce Bay in Scotland in 1937. The flowers of *Geranium s.* 'Glenluce' are well described as 'wild-rose pink', larger and softer coloured than the type. *G.s.* 'Jubilee Pink' and *G.s.* 'Shepherds Warning', also from Scotland, are much brighter – a rather more cerise-pink. These are two of the hybrids raised by Jack Drake at his Inshriach Nursery in Aviemore. At the Wisley trials they were awarded a First Class Certificate and a Highly Commended respectively.

All these forms of *Geranium sanguineum* have a habit of mounding themselves up into attractive humps, especially when grown in paving. The mounds of dark green leaves, spangled with the variously coloured flowers, look like wonderfully floral Christmas puddings.

A distinctive geranium for a front rank position is *Geranium renardii*. Its neat clump of sage-green leaves makes an excellent foil for the large, mallow-shaped flowers in palest mauve with darkly violet veins. Walter Ingwersen recommended growing it in similar conditions to its native habitat, on poor soil and between rocks, to maintain it in a compact form and to encourage flowering. Certainly the best specimen of this plant in my garden is growing in paving. An attractive companion would be *Alchemilla erythropoda*, a dainty plant with a similar but smaller leaf in bluish-green. Other plants to make a good grouping would include the steely-blue rue (*Ruta graveolens*), the angular stems, woolly grey leaves and round white flowers of *Lychnis coronaria alba*, and the brilliant contrast of *Potentilla* 'Gibson's Scarlet'.

The blue-flowered form of the geranium, *G. renardii* 'Whiteknights', is not in my opinion an improvement as it loses the delicate correlation of flower and leaf tones in the original plant.

It is probably best to avoid invidious comparisons, and treat it on its own merits as a good garden plant.

Herbs like lavender, marjoram and varieties of the culinary sage with coloured leaves would give good support, both physically and aesthetically, to species geraniums which are striking enough to warrant a star position in the front row, such as *Geranium oreganum* and *G. kishtvariense*. A sprinkling of the annual clary, *Salvia horminum*, with showy bracts in assorted colours, would add the finishing touch.

EXTENDING THE SEASON

Plants which prolong the flowering season into late summer and early autumn well deserve their space. Classic herbaceous plants such as *Phlox paniculata* in a whole range of rich colours are especially welcome. Admittedly, their stems and leaves are rather dull until the flowers appear, but this deficiency can be remedied by using them as a neutral background for such geraniums as *G. clarkei* 'Kashmir Purple', *G. collinum* and *G. erianthum*. Some of these may well still be flowering when the phlox season opens, and could also be interplanted amongst Michaelmas daisies (asters) to bridge a similar gap. The most reliably healthy species of asters are *Aster amellus* (in such favourite forms as *A.a.* 'King George' and *A.a.* 'Lac de Genève') and *Aster × frikartii*, especially *A. × f.* 'Mönch' and *A. × f.* 'Wunder von Stäfa', the blues and pale mauves of which would be compatible with most geraniums.

The exuberant semi-shrubby *Lavatera olbia* 'Rosea' is widely planted, and much appreciated for its heartwarming display of deep pink flowers all summer long and into autumn, accompanied throughout by *Geranium × oxonianum* 'Thurstonianum'. The paler, more refined version of the lavatera, *L.* 'Barnsley' is suitably underplanted with the various colour forms of *G. asphodeloides*, and the very aristocratic *G. aristatum* which has swept-back, stylishly striped petals.

However, the most useful plant for prolonged and varied interest is *Geranium wlassovianum*. The young leaves, with very distinctive chocolate-coloured central blotches on a rather olive-green background, start appearing in spring, an excellent foil to the deep violet-purple flowers in late summer. As these continue into the autumn, the older leaves start turning to fiery shades, but new leaves are still appearing in that distinguished dark green and brown. *G. wlassovianum*, allied with the harmonious colours of *Strobilanthes atropurpureus*, *Aster amellus* 'Violet Queen' and *Verbena hastata*, makes a very satisfactory late group, particularly if highlighted by the shocking pink annual *Silene armeria*.

Gardeners today are lucky to have available such a wide choice of plant material from all over the world. Combining plants in attractive associations is a fascinating exercise, to which geraniums can contribute a great deal. They blend so well with other plants that they are ideal for unifying groups and quickly making them look established.

UNDERPLANTING ROSES

Old roses and geraniums seem made for each other. This applies to species and shrub roses as well. The compact growth, generosity of flower and long-lasting foliage of the geraniums are just what is needed to complement the roses, which may have a fairly short flowering season. Sometimes they may also be rather sparsely furnished around the lower regions, and can benefit from a bit of herbaceous dressing-up.

Obviously their respective flower colours need to be taken into account, so that when their flowering seasons overlap they don't clash. Of course there is the theory that the occasional head-on clash does wonders to liven up the garden.

YELLOW ROSES

Playing safe, it is a general rule of thumb that the blue cranesbills assort well with yellow roses, especially the paler shades. Shrub roses like 'Nevada' and 'Frühlingsgold' which tend to have their main flush quite early in the season, are greatly enhanced by underplantings of *Geranium* × *magnificum*. *Rosa* 'Golden Wings' is a more compact, shrubby version of 'Mer-

maid' and works well in a mixed planting with other shrubs and perennials. Its long season is matched by that of *G*. 'Johnson's Blue'. The deeper tones of yellow, as in the English rose 'Graham Thomas' and the hybrid musk 'Buff Beauty' would be better partnered by the lighter blue geraniums – selected pale forms of *G. pratense*, or *G.p.* 'Mrs Kendall Clark'. The rugosa hybrid *R*. 'Agnes' is seldom seen, but always creates a lot of interest when in bloom. The fully double flowers in pale yellow, a richer tone at the centre, have a delicious scent but a shorter season than their full-blooded cousins. The deep violet-blue flowers of *G*. × *magnificum* throw their delicacy into even greater prominence, and after flowering the geranium leaves remain, for continuity of foliage interest.

PINK ROSES

When we come to pink roses, the decision is less straightforward, as many of the pink geraniums are not true pink but incline more towards the purple end of the spectrum. *G. endressii* might be a bit too strident teamed with *Rosa* 'New Dawn' for example; a better choice would be the hybrid *G*. × *oxonianum* 'Winscombe' with flowers that span the range from deep pink to silvery-pink. *G. endressii* 'Wargrave Pink', also in a softer tone, is usually described as salmon-pink, but in my view is more reminiscent of strawberry blancmange. Some of the deep blue geraniums could also tone with pink roses effectively, such as *G. ibericum*, *G. platypetalum* or the hybrids *G*. 'Brookside' and *G*. 'Spinners'.

RED ROSES

Many of the old roses have rich purple or dark red flowers, which would be shown off to advantage by the large, deep mauve flowers of *Geranium phaeum* 'Lily Lovell', together with the clear pink, white-veined flowers of *G. pratense* 'Bittersweet' – a much more definite colour than the wishy-washy pinks which sometimes appear amongst self-sown seedlings.

The rugosa roses are easy subjects for quite poor sandy soil. If left to their own devices they form rather gaunt bushes, but given the occasional hard cut-back they respond with good, new growth of lusty young stems bearing a heavy crop of more accessible flowers. *R.* 'Roseraie de L'Haÿ' is my particular favourite, for its length of flowering, rich colour and intoxicating fragrance. The double form of *Geranium himalayense, G.h.* 'Plenum' (also called 'Birch Double') makes an underlay that is equally sumptuous.

WHITE ROSES

The double white rugosa rose, *R.* 'Blanc Double de Coubert' is such a pure, dead white that it would be good to bring a little colour to its cheeks with an underplanting of *Geranium endressii*. Some of the taller varieties of G. × *oxonianum* could be used, or the ivory-white flowers of *G. pratense* forma *albiflorum* could provide a more subtle association with the rose.

White roses are easy of course – just about anything will go with them. Or will it? They all vary in degrees of whiteness – some are pink in the bud, some are creamy-white, some have a pinkish flush at maturity – so there is still scope for choosing a partner with a gentle affinity. For those with a trace of pink, *Geranium clarkei* 'Kashmir White' works well, by virtue of its pink veining and centre. This plant is low-growing, increasing gradually by underground rhizomes. Its informal habit offsets any rigidity in the shape of the rose bush. *Rosa* 'Iceberg' is still a great favourite, probably the most widely planted white rose, in spite of its occasional tendency to blackspot. Its pink-tinged bud is pointed up by *G. clarkei* 'Kashmir White', or for a closer cover and a warmer effect, the pastel pink flowers of *G. sanguineum* var. *striatum* backed by its thick mat of dark green leaves.

Formal rose gardens, as features, are not so often seen now, except in large-scale gardens. The purist would say that *any* underplanting would detract from them, even an edging. On the other hand, surely an edging of the right kind of plants would help to frame the bed, tie it into its surroundings, and maintain interest even when the roses were not in flower.

There are quite a few choices. *Geranium endressii* would provide a band of evergreen foliage and a long succession of flowers, but their bright pink might well 'swear' at the roses. *G. himalayense* is a better idea, especially in its 'Gravetye' form. *G. sanguineum* 'Album' is wonderfully neutral. For foliage interest, forms of *G. macrorrhizum* are excellent, providing the bonus of aromatic leaves and autumn tints. The colour of the flowers might be a problem, depending on which form was chosen. *G.m.* 'Ingwersen's Variety' complements most roses, while the richer-coloured flowers of *G.m.* 'Spessart' or *G.m.* 'Czakor' might be more difficult to place. The ideal compromise is *G.m.* 'Album' which would enhance anything without offending. There is quite a possibility in any case that the geraniums would have finished flowering before the rose season began, and any belated flowers would not be in sufficient quantity to cause an uproar.

Another possibility is to have alternating groups of several different geraniums around the perimeter of the rose bed. These could intermingle with contrasting foliage plants such as santolinas and *Teucrium chamaedrys*, although restricting it to one kind would probably be more effective.

All-over underplanting of a rose bed is not usually recommended as this restricts access for pruning and deadheading, and fertiliser given to the roses would inevitably lead to over-stimulation and excessive growth of the ground cover. However, any of the geraniums with trailing stems could be planted round the edge and encouraged to grow into the centre. *Geranium asphodeloides* in its various colour forms, *G. sanguineum* 'Album' and G. × *riversleaianum* 'Mavis Simpson' all provide flowery mats for long summer interest, and could then be trimmed back to their base.

PAGES 34–5
At Coombland Nursery the classic rose, *Rosa* 'Fantin-Latour' is well partnered by one of the newer hybrid geraniums, *G.* 'Spinners', with *G. albanum* providing background interest

36

GERANIUMS FOR
DRY SHADY PLACES

Dry shade in the garden presents a challenge. It may be shade from trees and shrubs in your own garden, 'borrowed' shade from plantings next door, or shade caused by shared walls and fences. The first step is to improve the soil by digging in compost or manure, with an occasional top sprinkling of a slow-release fertiliser – bearing in mind that the hungry roots of any trees in the vicinity will also enjoy this addition to their diet. Then choose your plants. There is a wide choice of plants which will tolerate and even enjoy shade and dryness, and will consequently keep the area as well furnished as the rest of the garden. In fact there is a great opportunity to give your shady ground its own individual character and attraction.

Geranium macrorrhizum provides the perfect solution, as it steadily increases into a leafy mat. In really tough conditions it will stay close to the ground, but in a less shady place, where it gets a little more light and the soil is less dry, it will rise up to over 12in (30cm) with bigger, lusher leaves, surmounted by flowers in white, pink or purple to give a truly opulent effect. The slightly clammy leaves have a distinct perfume, reminiscent of the Rose Geranium fragrance which is a popular ingredient in toiletries. At one time, oil of geranium was extracted from this plant, and after working amongst the plants, the scent persists on the hands. This is not to everyone's taste – or smell, and some visitors are not at all pleased when offered a crushed leaf to inhale. Robin Lane Fox thinks it smells of peppermint. Millar Gault says the scent is reminiscent of sweet briar, but more astringent.

At first glance it might appear that each leafy rosette is individually rooted; in fact the juicy rhizomatous stems often travel some distance from the central crown before taking root. However, propagation is easily effected by detaching a rosette with a short length of stem, and growing it on in a shaded nursery bed, where it will soon root and make a new plant. The leaves are bright green through the spring and summer,

but as autumn approaches they take on warm shades of red and orange to give interest during the winter. The wide open flowers with their lolling stamens are freely borne in late spring, sometimes with the bonus of a few more flowers late in the season.

The variety most often seen is *Geranium macrorrhizum* 'Ingwersen's Variety' in which the flowers are a clear sugar-pink. *G.m.* 'Bevan's Variety' has flowers of a rich rosy-red. Both of these are most effective when seen en masse, perhaps with a clump of *Geranium phaeum* or a group of mixed aquilegias to contrast in height and habit, with a spread of bergenias for another change in scale. The so-called 'white' form (*G. macrorrhizum* 'Album') is in reality the palest blush-pink. The contrasting brownish-red calyces and stems suggest that forms of digitalis would look effective alongside. *Digitalis*

'Ingwersen's Variety' is the most widely grown form of *G. macrorrhizum*. The aromatic leaves are good all year, colouring in autumn and supplemented by clear pink flowers in spring

ferruginea with brownish, white-lipped flowers, *D. × mertonensis*, the 'crushed strawberry' foxglove, or *D. purpurea* subsp. *heywoodii*, with creamy flowers and wonderfully soft leaves would all look marvellous.

For an area where the dry shade is caused by trees, and a more informal, natural look is wanted, *Geranium phaeum* comes into its own. A European plant introduced to Britain before the end of the sixteenth century, the common names are 'Dusky Cranesbill' or 'Mourning Widow', referring to the very dark red flowers which often appear near black in certain lights, or in other people's gardens! It has a rather flat, dark green leaf, divided into seven toothed lobes, each with a dark blotch. The flowers, which have a silky texture, are carried on erect stems and open over a long period, so plenty of seedlings are produced, often with some variations of flower colour. The pure white form, *Geranium phaeum album*, with bright golden anthers, contrasts well with the type and would make an interesting group with some of these seedling variations.

For foliage contrasts of different types, try *Asplenium scolopendrium* (Hart's Tongue fern), purple-leaved ajuga and *Tolmiea menziesii* 'Taff's Gold' (the variegated form of the pick-a-back plant) which has long, narrow flowers in a sinister shade of purple which would echo the colour of *G. phaeum*.

A similar geranium with very strongly spotted leaves used to be known as *Geranium punctatum*, but it has now been changed to *Geranium × monacense* 'Muldoon' in a rather unlikely homage to the Spotty Muldoon character in the legendary radio programme *The Goon Show*, starring the late Peter Sellers. A recent and even more confusing piece of nonsense has been to apply the name 'Muldoon' to a geranium with variegated leaves which is correctly known as *G. phaeum variegatum*. *Geranium × monacense* itself is closely allied to *G. phaeum*, except that the flowers, in various purples, reds and mauves, have a white centre surrounded by a dark blue ring which is darkly veined, and the flower itself is strongly reflexed. The detailing of the flower

and the mix of colour forms brings added interest to a dry shady place.

A very substantial and determined plant for ground cover in difficult areas is *Geranium × oxonianum* 'Claridge Druce' – but it is also the most dangerous. Once established it is difficult to dislodge as the many strong, spreading roots keep it well anchored, and a pickaxe often has to be brought into play. It makes a clump of dark green leaves up to 24in (61cm) with large purplish-pink flowers, heavily veined and very fertile, so that many seedlings appear in due course. It is fatal to allow these to reach flowering stage, as the many variations in size, colouring and veining of the flowers will persuade any soft-hearted gardener to allow them to take up permanent residence. However, for an isolated place in dry shade where nothing much else will grow, it makes an ideal understorey for trees and shrubs, and is a very handsome plant at all times of the year. Some tough plants of good size are needed to match the competition of this bulky geranium, such as common foxgloves and the deepest-purple form of honesty (*Lunaria annua*) you can find – the form with variegated leaves would be even better. The geranium was named after Dr George Claridge Druce (1850–1932), a chemist who became Mayor of Oxford and was a noted writer of several county *Floras*.

Geranium nodosum is much better behaved, and altogether on a smaller scale. It would be a shame to banish it entirely to the wilderness. Although it will thrive in dry shade, it is also very welcome in many other parts of the garden. The leaves are very distinctive, being shiny and five-lobed at the base of the plant, and can be mistaken at a quick glance for those of *Astrantia maxima*. The leaves borne on the 12in (30cm) flower stems are three-lobed, setting off the flowers which come and go all year. The square-ended petals are lilac-mauve with deep purple veining, and give rise to random seedlings which may have their own ideas about colour but are always acceptable. Good companion plants would be *Dicentra formosa*, with its dangling pink lockets on flesh-pink stalks and its ferny, glaucous leaves, and the similarly coloured *Dentaria digitata* (now *Cardamine pentaphyllos*) which vanishes after flowering, so the geranium would mark the spot.

Geranium versicolor is a small unassuming plant usually recommended for a woodland area or wild planting, but not to be despised. The light green leaves with characteristic light reddish-brown blotches between the divisions are good for most of the year. The off-white flowers, heavily veined in an intricate pattern, have given it such delightful nicknames as 'Painted Lady' and 'Queen Anne's Needlework'. E.A. Bowles and A.T. Johnson both knew it as *Geranium striatum*, and remarked on the mutual attraction it had for *Geranium endressii*.

In *My Garden in Summer* Bowles wrote, 'In many gardens these two fall in love at first sight and end in a matrimonial alliance that peoples their near neighbourhood with hybrid offspring. Rosy-grounded *Geranium striatum* and veined and pencilled *Geranium endressii* fledglings appear in endless varieties of pattern and shade'. In *A Garden in Wales*, Johnson's version of this was, 'Let the Pyrenean (*G. endressii*) get within beckoning distance of the Italian (*G. striatum*) and the pair go in for matrimony with such unrestrained enthusiasm that the world about them soon becomes peopled with their half-caste offspring. And very pretty some of these are'. Very pretty, but very confusing!

Geranium endressii is of course the ground coverer par excellence. Indestructible, evergreen and ever-flowering, its somewhat sideways habit of growth fits it for any nook or cranny. It is particularly effective as an underplanting for shrubs in dry shady positions or for filling in spaces between taller plants.

GERANIUMS FOR DRY SUNNY PLACES

Geranium malviflorum is a most desirable plant, bursting into large and brilliant flowers in spring, with little prior warning. These opulent blossoms of violet-blue with red veins are particularly arresting in comparison with the multitudes of other spring flowers in conventional yellow or white. It is ideal for growing in a dry sunny place, preferably south-facing, where it can provide a most exotic effect, especially if contrasted with the long-stemmed white daisy flowers of *Anthemis cupaniana*. This is an excellent plant for growing on a bank or a raised bed, where the low mats of small, ferny, blue-grey leaves will look good all winter, and spread out and trail down in summer. Regular deadheading will keep the flowers coming over a long period, even the odd one or two in winter.

Geranium malviflorum, colourful though it is in spring, has the inconvenient habit of dying down completely after flowering, leaving an empty space. Under the ground, the dark-skinned tubers, looking like oddly knobbly sausages, enjoy the summer baking which creates enough energy to send up leaves in autumn and flowers the following spring. The very finely cut leaves may look delicate but they are completely hardy. They make excellent ground cover all winter, undismayed by any weather.

In a shadier place, or under shrubs, the leaves appear on schedule but the flowers refuse to join them. This is understandable when you consider that the plant's previous name was *G. atlanticum*, a direct indication of its origin in the Atlas Mountains but a confusion to people who may have thought it had something to do with the Atlantic Ocean.

In a dry sunny position *Geranium malviflorum* associates well with helianthemums, the rock roses. Those with white or pale yellow flowers would be most effective, such as *Helianthemum* 'Wisley White', *H.* 'The Bride' or *H.* 'Wisley Primrose'. They bloom well into the summer, and having been tidied up by cutting the spent flower stalks right back, they continue the interest with neat mats of silvery-grey foliage. *Alyssum saxatile* would be another good spring partner, not the usual form which has mustard-yellow flowers, but the much softer *A.s.* var. *citrinum* or *A.s.* 'Silver Queen', with sprays of pastel yellow flowers over silvery leaves.

There are other part-time geraniums from exotic locations which enjoy an extended summer holiday while basking in the sun. *Geranium*

libani is from the Lebanon, and also has leaves which appear in autumn and are joined by flowers in spring. The leaves are not as finely cut as those of G. *malviflorum* and the flowers are smaller but still a good rich colour, with a rather puckered edge. Then there is G. *tuberosum* from the Mediterranean area, whose leaves and flowers appear simultaneously in spring. The leaves are finely divided and somewhat greyish. The small flowers on erect stalks are variable in colour but usually a pale purplish-pink.

The problem caused by these geraniums leaving a bare patch in summer can be easily solved by interplanting them with varieties such as *Geranium traversii* var. *elegans* and two of its hybrids. G. *traversii*, with silvery-grey leaves and pale pink flowers, comes from the Chatham Islands, some 400 miles east of New Zealand. Its hardiness can be doubtful, but it is well pleased with a hot, dry spot. Rather more reliable, but still glad of that favoured position, are the two hybrids between G. *traversii* and G. *endressii* –

G. *malviflorum* (formerly known as G. *atlanticum*) has large, dramatically coloured flowers in spring, but then becomes dormant until the new leaves appear in autumn. Here it is flourishing on a hot dry bank, contrasting with the white and silver of *Anthemis cupaniana* and *Helianthemum* 'Wisley White'

G. 'Russell Prichard' and G. 'Mavis Simpson'. These now come under the separate classification of G. × *riversleaianum*. This incorporates the name of the now defunct Riverslea Nursery at Christchurch in Hampshire, the first hybrid being named after a member of the Prichard family who ran it. (All too often in nursery catalogues a superfluous 't' appears in the surname, ie 'Pritchard' – even the Royal Horticultural Society's dictionary is guilty of this error.) The other cross from the same parentage, G. × *r.* 'Mavis Simpson' appeared spontaneously at the Royal Botanic Gardens at Kew some years later, and was named after a member of staff there.

Both plants are very good value, flowering endlessly all summer, the greyish-green leaves forming an excellent foil for the rosy-magenta flowers of *Geranium* × *r.* 'Russell Prichard' and the paler pink, white-flecked flowers of *G.* × *r.* 'Mavis Simpson'. One of the best examples of the latter I've seen was growing in a brick pavement, where it looked very happy and had spread into a wide circle.

For an autumn highlight, nerines provide wonderfully expensive-looking pink flowers, especially if the warmth and dryness of the area is augmented by a wall at their back. They tone in with another seasonal association – the pale purple flowers of *Geranium procurrens* weaving in and out of silvery-grey cistus bushes and smoky purple sage (*Salvia officinalis* 'Purpurascens'). Cistus and salvias are natural choices for hot, dry spots which are similar to the Mediterranean habitats where they originate. A bank or raised bed to accentuate the drainage would ensure that they overwintered easily.

Geranium × *riversleaianum* 'Russell Prichard' is a low-growing plant which forms a mat of silvery-grey leaves, studded with bright flowers

In such a favourable position it would be well worth trying the giant *Geranium maderense* from Madeira. Conventional advice is to grow it as a greenhouse plant, where it will take up a great deal of space and need constant repotting to keep it going without a check, but experiments with growing it outside in a sheltered situation where winters are mild have proved very successful. Basically, it looks like a hugely inflated *G. robertianum*, it can go up to 72in (1.5m) tall and wide in proportion, with spectacular leaves and a tremendous crop of purplish flowers, a richer colour at the centre, usually dying off after setting plentiful seed.

GERANIUMS FOR MOIST SHADY CORNERS

This is the sort of place where two varieties of geranium with variegated leaves could be displayed to advantage – both needing a richer, moister soil than their green-leaved forms.

Geranium phaeum 'Variegatum' makes a striking plant. The large leaves are randomly

marked with soft colour washes of pale greyish-green and cream on the basic dark green background, enlivened by the occasional red dot. The colour is always best on the new growth in spring, but will give a repeat performance in autumn if revitalised by a severe cut-back in summer. There is a splendid example in 'Bowles' Corner' at the Royal Horticultural Society's garden at Wisley, Surrey. Here there is a collection of plants which were favourites of the garden writer and plantsman E.A. Bowles, who was particularly interested in unusual and aberrant specimens.

Some people do not find *Geranium macror-rhizum* 'Variegatum' as easy to grow as the other members of its family. The soft leaves are pale green with good creamy markings, but maybe it hasn't got enough chlorophyll in its veins to give it the energy for running about too much. It needs quite a lot of encouragement in the way of feeding and watering before it will settle down and look happy, but it will reward the little extra attention. It would be as well if the surrounding

The variegated form of *G. macrorrhizum* needs a little more care and attention than its relatives to give of its best. It is beautifully grown here in a moist shady corner of a Lincolnshire garden, with the contrasting foliage of hostas and pulmonarias, and a ground-hugging carpet of *Ajuga reptans* 'Variegata'

plants did not compete in variegation but furnished a complete contrast in form and texture to the two geraniums.

A good grouping would include: *Pulmonaria rubra* ('Christmas cowslip') which flowers from mid-winter for several months, then provides a fresh array of plain, light green leaves till next autumn; *Iris foetidissima* with bottle-green, sword-like leaves bending demurely at the tips, and pods of bright orange berries for autumn and

PAGES 42–3
In a damp shady spot, *Geranium* x *magnificum* is accompanied by candelabra primulas in a range of soft colours, with vertical contrast provided by iris foliage and the strong leaves of *Lysichiton americanus*. A good alternative choice of geranium for this area would be *G. maculatum*

44

winter attraction; and *Tiarella cordifolia*, a friendly little plant which quietly goes about making a colony of vine-shaped leaves to set off the fluffy white flower spikes in summer. Depending on the size of the shady corner bed, a number of other stylish leaf forms could be added, such as *Helleborus foetidus* or *H. orientalis*, hostas in variety, *Heuchera cylindrica* 'Greenfinch' and some of the smaller, neater-growing forms of epimedium – all designed to show off and flatter the two leading ladies.

GERANIUMS FOR GRAVEL OR SCREE BEDS

Many of the smaller geraniums respond well to growing on sharply drained beds, being given more space than they would get in a sink or container, and thus making better plants. Even in a small garden it is usually possible to construct a separate gravel area, which will not only give an opportunity to develop a style of planting which

The basal growth of G. *cinereum* var. *cinereum* is dwarfed by the size of the strongly-veined flowers. This variety is ideal for sinks or scree

is quite distinct from the rest of the garden, but will also allow the geraniums in particular to be displayed to their best advantage.

On a rather larger site there would be room for a scree bed, which is usually constructed with coarser material, often on a slight slope but necessarily in a sunny position. There is an excellent one at Hault Farm in Kent, which was converted from an old ha-ha. I saw it not long after the transformation; the plants, including many geraniums, had quickly settled in and were obviously enjoying their new quarters.

The scree or gravel bed is a development from the rockery which at one time was a standard garden feature but which is quite difficult to construct and plant convincingly. These new mini-landscapes are much more informal, and have the advantage that the whole area is surfaced with gravel, from which annual weeds are easily removed. Obviously, any perennial weeds must be completely eradicated before the construction is started. Conversely, the gravel also forms an ideal medium into which alpines and other desirable garden plants will sow themselves freely. The seedlings enjoy the open texture from which excess moisture drains, while still keeping their roots damp and cool. It is then simply a question of sorting the sheep from the goats, or the wheat from the chaff!

A superb example of this type of construction is the extensive 'Dry Garden' in the Savill Garden at Windsor Great Park. Created on a large sloping site which was naturally dry, huge amounts of gravel quarried elsewhere on the estate were incorporated into it. Part of the ground is shaded by trees, giving an opportunity to vary the planting, but most of the area is open and sunny. Nearly forty species and cultivars of hardy geraniums are now flourishing there, together with many interesting varieties of erodiums, euphorbias, shrubby potentillas, kniphofias, artemisias, schizostylis, bulbs and a rich mix of other shrubs and perennials. There is a huge specimen of *Geranium incanum* var. *multifidum*, a South African native which is not the easiest plant to keep going. There have been several unsuccessful attempts to overwinter it in my garden in Surrey, but at the Savill Garden in autumn it had made a wonderfully frothy mat of finely divided, silvery leaves, still lavishly dotted with clear purple flowers.

Geranium cinereum 'Ballerina' was also featured there. Larger than its parents, it has a good helping of grey-green leaves and an extended season of subdued purplish-pink flowers, charmingly veiled with dark veins. A nice contrast in texture and habit would be the smallest and neatest of the cotton lavenders, *Santolina chamaecyparissus* 'Weston', coupled with one of the smaller, purple-leaved sedums such as *S*. × 'Ruby Glow' or the trailing *S*. 'Bertram Anderson'. Even without the geranium's other undoubted attractions, the sheer glamour of the name 'Ballerina' would make it very popular.

Geranium cinereum 'Ballerina' has a sibling, *G.c.* 'Lawrence Flatman'. They both come from the same cross (*G. cinereum* var. *cinereum* × *G.c.* var. *subcaulescens*) and both were introduced by Blooms of Bressingham, in 1963 and 1979 respectively. *G.c.* 'Lawrence Flatman' is more assertive – one might almost say masculine – with larger, deeper-coloured flowers, each petal having a darker mark which gives the impression of a striped flower. The two varieties are quite easily confused when seen separately, especially as the distinctive marking on the 'Lawrence Flatman' flower may vary somewhat with soil and situation. The large open flowers of *Campanula carpatica* 'White Clips' or the subtle blue-grey colouring of *C.c.* 'Blue Moonlight' would assort with it well. So would *Sisyrinchium* 'May Snow', rising from a low clump of leaf-fans, with a much longer flowering period than its name would imply.

The gravel bed is an ideal site for *Geranium sessiliflorum* subsp. *novaezelandiae* 'Nigricans', a connoisseur's plant if ever there was one. You either love or loathe its low-key attraction. The closely packed rosettes of small, dark browny-bronze leaves may be highlighted by the random production of an occasional bright orange leaf, but unless carefully positioned it can melt into the background. Gravel or paving can show it off successfully, provided the colour and texture of

the material are right. When happy, the geranium will seed around mildly, the seedlings often varying in leaf colour. One variety has a more distinct appearance, with rich, dark red leaves. The usual form, however, presents a challenge in finding suitable plant associations.

This can be tackled from several angles. One solution is to put it next to low-growing plants with gold or variegated leaves. These might include: *Lysimachia nummularia* 'Aurea' with bright gold leaves and matching flowers; *Veronica prostrata* 'Trehane' with golden leaves and intense blue flowers; the variegated arabis, *A. caucasica* 'Variegata' or the flatter, mattier *A. ferdinandi-coburgii* 'Aureovariegata'.

For a geographical tie-up, use one of the bronze New Zealand grasses, *Carex buchananii* or *C. comans*, which will add height and definition to the group. Or go to the other extreme and accentuate the sombre colouring of the geranium leaves by surrounding them with the black grass *Ophiopogon planiscapus* 'Nigrescens',

G. cinereum 'Lawrence Flatman' is a more assertive, masculine plant than its sibling, *G. c.* 'Ballerina'. The cushion of dark grey-green leaves offsets the large open rose-purple flowers, each with a darker central zone to the petals that gives the impression of a striped flower

The shiny red-edged leaves of G. *dalmaticum* are up-staged by the clear pink flowers, here well contrasted with the cobweb sempervivum

habit of moulding itself over any odd stone or piece of tufa which may be near it, but it loses its leaves in winter, when it has been said to resemble old coconut matting. Sempervivums make good permanent companions for it, especially any which are red-flushed to echo the ruddy touches of the geranium leaves.

Other treasures to gloat over in a container or sink are *Geranium cinereum* and G. *argenteum* with ashy-green and silvery-green leaves respectively. Together they have produced several even more refined and desirable hybrids which come under the heading of G. × *lindavicum*. My own favourite among these is G. × *lindavicum* 'Apple Blossom', a very apt name since the large, palest pink and white flowers do seem to recapture the spring-time appeal of the first fruit tree blossom. Such a delicate plant needs something with a more solid form and texture to accompany it. *Sedum spathulifolium* 'Cappa Blanca' ('Cape Blanco') is a good

purple ajuga, the purple clover *Trifolium repens* 'Purpurascens' and, finally, *Viola labradorica* with its dark purplish-green leaves and its slaty-blue flowers.

GERANIUMS FOR SINKS AND CONTAINERS

Sinks and containers provide ideal growing conditions for most of the alpine varieties of geraniums, which require sharp drainage and sun. The very small varieties benefit by being raised nearer to eye level, so that the intricate detail of their leaves and flowers can be studied more easily.

Geranium dalmaticum is a case in point. The very neat, shiny leaves have a dark red outline all summer and go fiery-red in the autumn, providing a striking accompaniment to the surprisingly large sugar-pink flowers. There is also a pure white form but it seems a little more reluctant to flower. The compact plant has an endearing

choice, but the flat heads of bright yellow flowers are best removed as soon as possible.

Geranium farreri is a classic example of the miniaturist's art. Botanically it is in a class of its own, though there is a superficial resemblance to *G. argenteum*. It takes its name from the intrepid plantsman Reginald Farrer who discovered it in China in 1917 and waxed lyrical about it in his book *On the Eaves of the World*, writing about 'its profusion of large and very pale pink flowers . . . its faintly flushing blossoms, silvery in the cold pale air'. The exquisite leaves and flowers are well offset by *Achillea argentea*, with its rosettes of finely toothed leaves and long-lasting heads of white daisy flowers.

In brilliant, even strident contrast, is *Geranium cinereum* var. *subcaulescens*, in which the magenta and black flower colour of *G. psilostemon* is repeated and even intensified by its concentration into a smaller form. You don't

G. *cinereum* var. *subcaulescens* is distinguished by the intense colour of its black-eyed flowers, like a scaled-down version of G. *psilostemon*

The very delicate pale pink and white flowers give the apt name of 'Apple Blossom' to this form of G. × *lindavicum*. The shining silver leaves are inherited from one of its parents, G. *argenteum*

expect so small a plant to pack such a mighty punch, so take the opportunity to soften the impact by considered use of contrasting or toning foliage such as *Sempervivum* 'Othello' and the silky wigs of *Artemisia lanata* (now *A. caucasica*).

GERANIUMS FOR ROUGH GRASS

Although usually grown successfully in ordinary garden soil, both *Geranium pratense* (meaning 'of meadows') and *G. palustre* (meaning 'marsh loving') show by their names that they have an affinity with moister situations that are not too shady. Another kindred spirit would be *Geranium sylvaticum*, which often grows wild on river banks. Both *G. pratense* and *G. palustre* make good clumps; the latter's petals are more pointed and are usually bright pink. The wild form of *G. sylvaticum* is lavender-blue but it is

G. 'Philippe Vapelle'

G. *renardii*

G. 'Chantilly'

G. *robustum*

G. 'Nimbus'

G. *clarkei*
'Kashmir Purple'

G. *phaeum*
'Variegatum'

G. *macrorrhizum* 'Album'

G. *macrorrhizum*
'Variegatum'

G. *nodosum*

G. 'Ann Folkard'

G. *himalayense*

very variable. There are some good selected forms, especially *G. sylvaticum* 'Mayflower' which has rich violet-blue flowers accentuated by a distinct white centre. Any of the above would look good in rough grass with naturalised daffodils where the foliage would be helpful in camouflaging the dying leaves of the bulbs.

Other plants to group with the geraniums would be meadow-sweet, particularly in its golden-leaved form (*Filipendula ulmaria* 'Aurea'), and purple loosestrife (*Lythrum salicaria*) with its slender spires of brilliant flowers which continue for weeks on end in summer. *Geranium collinum* is another easy-going plant which would be happy in this situation.

A FAMILY GROUP

Useful and versatile as geraniums are for associating and blending with other plants, there is also a strong case for devoting a whole area to them on their own. This would not be in any sense a plantsman's garden, with each plant carefully labelled and separated from the others, but an informal planting, to demonstrate the affinities and differences which are present within any family group.

There is already the nucleus of such a grouping within my own garden. An area of poor soil in semi-shade underneath golden privet and forsythia, formed part of my 'desperation gardening' policy, where things were put in for quick effect and to deter weeds. Some spare plants of *Geranium* × *oxonianum* were used, with some self-sown seedlings of *G. versicolor*, showing variable characteristics. These have increased well, growing into each other, and some other hybrids have introduced themselves, including a medium-height variation of *G. psilostemon*. The intertwining stems mean that the various coloured flowers mix and mingle in a rather cottagey way.

This has led me to thinking of extending the idea to narrow borders on either side of a path through light woodland. There would be scope here for including a whole range of colours – from the blues of *Geranium pratense* and *G.*

himalayense, and the purple of *G. psilostemon*, to the various pinks of *G. endressii* and the *G.* × *oxonianum* hybrids. Along the path edge, *G. sanguineum* would provide clumps of deep green leaves and rich crimson flowers, intermingled with *Geranium macrorrhizum*. The flowering season of this multi-coloured display would be lengthened and enhanced by the semi-shaded location, and within a short time the plants would grow into each other to make a completely weedproof cover. Extra interest, and another variation in habit, would be provided by occasional plants of *Geranium sylvaticum* in both its 'Album' and 'Mayflower' forms, plus *G. phaeum* and *G.* × *monacense*.

Such a scheme would also work well with a new garden, or a neglected one which had just been taken over, where quick cover was needed without a great deal of preparation or maintenance. It would be much more rewarding in the long term than the mass planting of annuals which is sometimes recommended. Even if the plants had to be bought in initially, rather than bringing together existing plants from groups scattered around the garden, it should be possible to divide them up before planting out, to encourage them to establish quickly. Once the initial planting had settled down, it would form the basis of an ongoing scheme into which some of the newer hybrids such as *Geranium* 'Brookside' and *G.* 'Spinners' could be introduced as they were acquired. It would be an exercise in discipline as much as anything else, to resist the temptation of incorporating plants of other kinds and rely instead on the continually absorbing interest of the similarities and variance within one plant family.

GERANIUMS FOR FOLIAGE EFFECT

Geranium leaves are a continual delight throughout the year as they develop and change over the seasons. They could almost merit a book on their own, as their variations are so numerous and pleasing. But in a booklet about geraniums issued by the Northern Horticultural

Society, Melvyn Crann summed up the whole range beautifully in just one paragraph:

> The variety of geranium leaf forms is such that one could imagine that a class of art students had been set the task of designing as many leaf patterns as possible within the confines of a circle: there seems to be every possible variation – broadly lobed, lacily divided, trifid, almost completely circular, large, small, and in colours and textures ranging through light green, dark green, yellow, grey, brown, mottled, blotched, variegated, hairy, glossy, velvety and often pleasantly scented – a plant for all seasons.

SPRING

In spring there is the excitement of seeing new growth appearing every day. Geraniums are quite precocious and soon furnish the ground. Some self-sown seedlings of *Geranium endressii* and its hybrids may show promise of variegation, or at least a pale edging to the leaves, but unfortunately this vanishes as they mature. The new leaves of *G. dahuricum* however are reliably coloured with pink and yellow. *G. × monacense* 'Muldoon' (formerly *G. punctatum*) will have the occasional new leaf of primrose-yellow, throwing the dark spots into greater relief.

Geranium pratense quickly makes big leafy clumps which can be used to advantage in helping to disguise the leaves of spring bulbs as these die down. The strong, glossy leaves of colchicums, appearing months after their 'autumn crocus' flowers, are spectacular when new, but once they start deteriorating it takes an embarrassingly long time for them to make a graceful exit. The problem can be solved by interplanting them with *G. pratense* whose burgeoning new leaves will help to screen those of the colchicums. The geranium will flower around midsummer, after which it can be cut to the ground to encourage it to produce a fresh fountain of leaves as a graceful accompaniment to the naked colchicum flowers in autumn.

SUMMER

In summer everything is looking very lush, most of the geraniums contributing not only an assortment of flowers, but also an astonishing range of leaves.

A recently introduced cultivar, *Geranium* 'Walter's Gift' has particularly outstanding foliage. The plant is a cross between *G. × oxonianum* 'Claridge Druce' and *G. versicolor*. The leaves are a much more strongly coloured version of the latter, with the vigour of the former. The young leaves appear with a suffusion of light reddish-brown which becomes a darker colour as the leaf expands to a good size. Sometimes there is also a distinct matching spot on each of the leaf divisions. The contrast with the shiny green of the rest of the leaf is very striking, especially as the plant makes a sizeable clump and the leaves stay in good condition for some time.

Among the generous assortment of leaf shapes and shades in summer, two other geraniums might be singled out for special attention. My favourite of all is *Geranium renardii* which makes a compact mat of highly original leaves. They are crimped and scalloped, with a netted, tactile surface in soft grey-green, and would be a great asset to any garden even without the bonus of the flowers. Two interesting new hybrids have some of its blood in their veins – *G.* 'Chantilly' (*G. renardii* × *G. gracile*) and *G.* 'Philippe Vapelle' (*G. renardii* × *G. platypetalum*) both retain the shape of the *G. renardii* leaves, but in light green and dark grey-green respectively.

Geranium orientalitibeticum is a small plant with big ambitions. Why do some of the smallest plants have the longest names? The dainty leaves are deeply cut and marbled in two shades of green with yellow highlights. (It is often confused with *G. pylzowianum* which has more finely divided leaves in plain green.) Although delicate in appearance, *G. orientalitibeticum* is capable of rapid increase by the multiplication of its strange bead-like roots, and should definitely not be introduced to a rockery full of little treasures. However, if it is given a place where there is a bit of elbow room, perhaps a narrow bed alongside a path, it would look charming as an underplanting for something

G. wallichianum
'Buxton's Variety' (stem leaf)

G. wlassovianum

G. x *cantabrigiense*

G. collinum

G. pogonanthum

G. x *oxonianum* 'Walter's Gift'

G. dalmaticum

G. cataractarum

G. sessiliflorum
novaezelandiae
(red-leaved form)

G. magnificum

G. pulchrum

G. sanguineum 'Cedric Morris'

G. rubifolium

52

that grows with a substantial and definite outline, such as *Sedum spectabile* 'Iceberg' or *Sisyrinchium striatum* (now called *Phaiophleps nigricans*).

AUTUMN

The autumn colour of geranium leaves is, like that of trees and shrubs, very dependent on weather and soil conditions. Some varieties achieve a blaze of glory before dying down until the spring, others have leaves which change colour but are retained during the winter. This is the case with *Geranium macrorrhizum* and its varieties, except for *G.m.* 'Variegatum' which will die down without changing colour.

The brilliant hues of most deciduous varieties are fairly short-lived, especially if subjected to heavy autumn rain. Of the smaller plants, *Geranium sanguineum* and its various forms are the most spectacular. They have the advantage that their leaves are carried all along the flowering stems, which are often raised at an angle. The leaves themselves are intricately cut, and decrease in size along the stem, so they already look ornamental. The addition of autumn colouring, ranging through shades of red to gold, emphasises and dramatises this filigree effect, so they look like sprays of burning snow crystals. The hybrid *G.s.* 'Max Frei' seems a particularly good form in this respect.

The miniature leaves of *Geranium dalmaticum*, which are delightfully edged with red in summer, now turn completely red, especially after they have been touched by frost. The heraldic leaves of *G. psilostemon* turn deep red for a short but splendid season. The solid clumps of *G. magnificum* leaves turn from everyday dark green to frivolous pink and yellow. *G.* × *monacense* 'Muldoon' reverts to its spring mode, the dark spots becoming more prominent again on a pale yellow background. With *G. wallichianum* and its form *G.w.* 'Buxton's Variety', reddish touches on the mottled dark green leaves give a new dimension to the

flowers, which are still appearing. Other good-looking foliage colour comes from *G. erianthum* in pink, yellow and green, *G. platyanthum* and *G. wlassovianum*. *G. nodosum*, which has very distinctive leaves anyway, has their texture and veining accentuated as the shiny green surface gradually turns red.

WINTER

After the brilliant firework displays of the autumn foliage, overwintering geraniums revert to more ordinary dress; but there is a more subtle interest to be had from the diverse shapes and shades of green. The days may be dull but there is still a lot of life in the garden.

The delicate-looking leaves of *Geranium malviflorum* which appeared in autumn have now settled down for the winter. Undeterred by any bad weather, they are joined by two others resurrected after summer dormancy – *G. libani* and *G. peloponnesiacum*. Such well-established and reliable geraniums as *G. endressii*, *G. phaeum* and *G. versicolor* maintain their overwintering foliage in a variety of styles. *G.* × *o.* 'Claridge Druce' which has had to be forcibly restrained during the summer is now valued for its energetic display of dark green, dark-spotted leaves. *G. albanum* and *G. pyrenaicum*, likewise deplored for their earlier extravagance, are now welcomed to the winter scene.

The neat rosettes of *Geranium cataractarum* have a family resemblance to the larger red-stemmed growth of *G. robertianum*, which can be intriguingly variable in its detail. The narrowly divided grey-green leaves of *G. robustum*, quite sparsely held on angular stems, look more like one of the sophisticated, scented pelargoniums than a geranium. In spite of its name this plant is not reliably hardy, but will usually keep some of its leaves over winter and will occasionally produce a self-sown seedling. However, the prize for continuity of interest must go to *G. macrorrhizum*, which keeps its leaves going in various transformations throughout the year.

3
CULTIVATION

One of the main reasons for the increasing popularity of geraniums is that they are so easy to cultivate, giving excellent results for the maximum period of time with the minimum of maintenance.

SOIL AND SITUATION

Whatever their place of origin they are adaptable to a wide range of growing conditions and soils, whether acid or alkaline, making them especially valuable for chalk gardens and dry places. The situation is more important than the soil, though even here the guidelines are very broad and plants which in nature grow in damp situations will flourish quite happily in an ordinary garden.

The larger-growing varieties require little attention once established. The smaller kinds are loosely classed as alpines, although they may well originate from other mountainous regions such as the Himalayas, so should more correctly be referred to as 'montane' varieties. These do require a little more individual care at first, mainly in the choice of site. Most of them are happiest in sunny, well-drained positions. The area around each plant should be top-dressed with gravel, and an extra gravel mulch put on in the autumn. This will protect the roots in winter and ensure that there is no standing water around the neck of the plant, which could cause it to freeze and rot. In very severe weather it is well worth putting a small cloche, a sheet of glass or even a large upturned jam jar over any newly introduced plants of this type. It is also important to check regularly that neighbouring plants are not encroaching on them.

PLANTING

The optimum time for planting is between early autumn and early spring, depending on local conditions, when the soil is in a receptive state and the weather is without extremes.

Dig a generous hole to accommodate the plant comfortably. A mature plant of the larger varieties will usually have extensive roots, which should not be cramped. Prepare the planting hole by adding well-rotted garden compost or moistened peat to the existing soil, to give the plant a good start and encourage it to settle in. Manure is not necessary, in fact it will encourage the plant to become too lush and floppy, but a sprinkling of a slow-release fertiliser will be beneficial. On heavy ground, it is worth adding some sharp grit or perlite to improve the drainage – the one thing that geraniums dislike is a waterlogged soil.

Firm the plant in carefully and water it well. Make sure it does not dry out while it is becoming established. Taller varieties may need staking initially in case they are rocked and distorted by wind.

GENERAL CARE

With the larger varieties, a common complaint is that they seed around too much, or look untidy towards the end of the season, when their main flowering period is over. There is a simple solution to both problems – cut them back! If done in time, this will take off the seedheads before they have had a chance to ripen, and will also encourage the plants to renew themselves with a fresh crop of leaves, to keep them looking presentable for the rest of the season. They are then more likely to retain these leaves during the winter. The species which are most obliging in this way include *Geranium pratense, G. endressii, G. × oxonianum, G. × monacense, G. sylvaticum, G. asphodeloides, G. phaeum, G. himalayense* and *G. × magnificum*. In addition, all except the latter two will often produce a second crop of flowers. *G. endressii* in particular, that most industrious member of the genus, will certainly benefit from taking a summer breather once its first fine flush of flowers is tapering off, and will go into a repeat performance with renewed enthusiasm.

Geranium pratense, if grown in a sunny spot, may well start to flag and flop in a prolonged drought, and unless kept well watered may be susceptible to mildew. Cutting right back and watering well is the solution.

Geranium wallichianum 'Buxton's Variety', if grown in too hot a spot, will react by producing flowers in an indeterminate colour between purple and the usual true blue. This is a cry for help which can be answered by regular watering, twice a day if necessary. The long term solution would be to move it to a shadier place altogether.

Although *Geranium macrorrhizum* is always recommended as being ideal for poor, dry soils, it seems a shame to take it for granted and not give it a bit of encouragement from time to time. A few handfuls of good garden compost mixed with a little slow-release fertiliser, scattered through the top growth and gently brushed in, will be greatly appreciated.

PESTS AND DISEASES

One of the advantages of growing geraniums is the fact that they are virtually trouble free. Healthy plants are much less susceptible to pests and diseases than ailing ones. By dividing large clumps, keeping the soil in reasonable condition and removing dead and rotting debris, most problems can be prevented. The question of whether to use pesticides and fungicides, or organic methods, is a matter of personal choice. In any case, poisonous chemicals should be used with great restraint.

Slugs and Snails: These pests are always with us, but damage to geranium foliage is usually minimal. Very occasionally succulent seedlings (always the most precious ones) provide an appetising hors d'oeuvre for these marauders. Strategically placed slug pellets, preferably the organic type, can be used to provide distraction and destruction, or apply your own patent remedy.

Aphids: These rarely attack cranesbills in the open ground, but white fly can be a nuisance in the greenhouse. Leaves become covered with sticky honeydew, and later a black, sooty mould. *Geranium canariense* and its relations are favourite hosts. Aphids are difficult to control, and unless you can persuade hoverflies to do the job, spraying with a proprietary insecticide at regular intervals will be necessary.

Vine Weevils: These are a much more serious problem. Plants in pots are most at risk, especially in damp, soil-less compost. The adult beetle is dark greyish-brown with a snout. They are all female, as males are not required for reproduction. They feed nocturnally on foliage, resting during daylight hours in well-camouflaged comfort on the soil, where they lay vast quantities of eggs over a period of two to three months. The larvae, usually apparent from midsummer onwards, are small, creamy-white grubs with orange heads, curled up in a circle and growing fat on juicy roots. Wilted, sickly looking foliage is the first sign of their presence. Lift and inspect the plants. If grubs are found, but the roots are not totally destroyed, wash off all the soil with a liquid insecticide such as BHC or malathion, and make sure all the grubs are taken out and killed. Dispose of all the old compost safely, scrub the containers, and repot the plants in fresh potting compost. Dusting the surface of the compost with BHC or malathion powder helps to deter the adults from egg laying, or try a good layer of grit or chippings. The beetles are very persistent, however, and regular inspection and treatment is advisable. Plants in the open ground can be dealt with in the same way, but control is more difficult.

G. *sanguineum* 'Max Frei'

G. *sanguineum* 'Cedric Morris'

G. *sanguineum* 'Jubilee Pink'

G. *sanguineum* var. *striatum*

G. 'Dilys'

G. x *riversleaianum* 'Mavis Simpson'

G. x *oxonianum* 'Rose Clair'

G. *pratense* (pale blue form)

G. *phaeum* 'Lily Lovell'

G. *phaeum*

G. *palustre*

56

It is generally agreed that these pests are much more prevalent since the use of peat-based potting composts has become more widespread. Good results have been obtained by turning to composts based on coco fibre, either a proprietary brand or mixed with a loam-based compost, although these do require more care in watering. There is also a biological control in the form of a natural predator called heterorhabditis; it is sold as Nemasys and Bio-Safe.

Rust: This disease sometimes manifests itself as raised yellow, orange or rust-brown spots on the foliage.

Affected leaves should be picked off and destroyed. Spraying with a special rust control at fortnightly intervals should clear up the trouble, but if it continues it is best to destroy the plant.

Powdery Mildew: This is a white, mealy growth which appears on the leaves, usually in very dry or overcrowded conditions. Some forms of *Geranium pratense* are rather prone to it.

Cut all the foliage right down and burn it to prevent the spread of spores. Give the plant a good soaking, a handful of general fertiliser and dust it with Flowers of Sulphur, or water with a fungicide. Recovery is good, but the mildew may recur, particularly in a drought situation.

Virus: This occasionally infects species such as *G. rubescens* and other geraniums of this group, causing distortion of the flowers. Destroy afflicted plants as there is no known cure. The virus can be transferred to future generations through the seed. Any seedlings showing signs of flower distortion should also be eradicated.

4

PROPAGATION

Quite a few gardeners tell me that they never read the chapter on propagation in gardening books. Experienced gardeners have probably evolved their own individual routines over the years, while new gardeners may think it is a complicated business with which they do not want to bother at the moment. But please read on – we believe this chapter could interest *all* gardeners. Even the most experienced should compare notes with Allan Robinson's expert advice on dealing with the less straightforward alpine varieties – and if you have never propagated a plant in your life, start with geraniums and you will be delighted with your success rate.

DIVISION

Most of the perennial geraniums are very easy to propagate by division. Mature plants of such species as *Geranium endressii* and its hybrids, G. *pratense*, G. *phaeum*, and G. *sylvaticum* will usually supply rather more divisions than you know what to do with. Each piece with a root and a shoot is capable of making a nice new plant quite readily.

With *Geranium phaeum* it will be found that the rhizomatous roots at the centre of a large clump will start to deteriorate, become woody and crumble away after a few years, so division is necessary to maintain the health and productivity of the plant. All the species named above make their best impression when seen en masse, so when a large clump has been split, the divisions can be replanted quite close together to repeat the effect.

The dormant period between late autumn and early spring is usually recommended as the best time for division, but I find that just after flowering, when the plant has been cut back, is very suitable for the operation. Divisions lined out then will make reasonable plants for a good show the next year.

CUTTINGS

There are some geraniums, like G. *wallichianum*, G. 'Ann Folkard' and G. 'Salome' which produce a lot of trailing stems, but they originate from a rootstock which is surprisingly small, and takes a long time to bulk up enough to be divided. In this case, cuttings are the answer. Side shoots of new growth taken in spring can be carefully removed with a sharp knife and potted up in a soil-based compost with extra grit added. At a later stage, one of the long trailing stems can be cut into pieces, each piece containing a node (the section where the leaves join the stem) which is then potted up so that the node is just above the compost. In both cases they should be shaded from the sun, with overhead watering from a fine spray to keep them moist until well rooted, when they can be potted on.

ROOT CUTTINGS

The double forms of *Geranium pratense*, being sterile, can either be propagated by division or root cuttings. In fact both operations can be carried out at the same time. A mature plant will have several crown buds coming from quite a woody rootstock, surrounded by a mass of thick and tangled roots. The crown has literally to be sawn apart with something like an old bread knife, leaving each division with its own crown

58

bud. In the process, some of the roots will inevitably become damaged or detached. After trimming up, the best of these can be used as root cuttings, being either potted up or inserted directly into a nursery bed.

There are other cases, such as *Geranium malviflorum* and *G. orientalitibeticum*, where the plants obligingly produce tuberous roots which can be detached and grown on. During the summer dormancy of *G. malviflorum*, these roots will often rise up to the surface of the ground or just below it. They are long, narrow and knobbly with dark brown skins – in general appearance not unlike the 'Pink Fir Apple' variety of salad potato. In the case of *G. orientalitibeticum* and the closely related *G. pylzowianum*, the tuberous roots are small, more rounded and pink in colour, like little strings of ethnic beads.

SEED

Seed may be obtained by joining a specialist society such as the Hardy Plant Society or the Alpine Garden Society and participating in their seed exchange schemes, or buying it from

G. asphodeloides has an endearing habit of trailing its long flowering stems over or through other plants. The widely separated petals give a starry effect, and self-sown seedlings come in a variety of pastel shades

specialised seed firms such as Chiltern Seeds. You can, of course, collect your own from plants already growing in the garden. On one hand, the result may not be entirely true to type, on the other hand there is the possibility of raising a new hybrid! Quite a few species will come true from seed, provided there are no other compatible species around, but such kinds as *Geranium endressii* and *G. pratense* are notoriously promiscuous and will probably come up with quite a few variations.

In any case, the first step is to catch your seed! With some plants, the ripe seed is retained for some time before being scattered, but geraniums tend to disperse it just as soon as it is ripe.

The swollen seed pods are said to resemble the bill of a crane, hence the common name of cranesbill. In most cases they split open from the bottom into five sections, each carrying a seed, which then either drops to the ground or is thrown some distance away, depending on the dispersal mechanism of that particular species. Constant vigilance is necessary to harvest the seed before the capsule bursts. Generally the seed pod changes colour from green to brown, which is the sign of ripeness, but there are various degrees of colour depending on the particular species. Luckily most varieties flower and therefore set seed over quite a long period, so there is a chance to check it at various stages of development, and gain experience of the crucial signs. *Geranium wallichianum* 'Buxton's Variety' is a good example, producing new flowers at one end of the trailing stem while seed is ripening at the other end. Daily inspection is essential. If you are not quite sure, tying a small paper bag (not plastic) or a small piece of muslin over the seedhead will make sure the ripe seed is retained for your collection.

A member of the Hardy Geranium Group writes of his success in delaying the seed ejection by pinching off the very tip of the 'beak' so that the explosive dispersal device is removed, and the seed can be collected in your own time.

As a general principle, seed of hardy plants that you collect yourself is best sown as soon as ripe, as it would be in nature. Storing in a paper bag in a warm place for a few days will ensure that it is completely ripe. Autumn sowing does assume that the gardener will have the facilities to overwinter the seedlings under some protection. If not, it would be advisable to delay sowing until the spring. Quite a lot of geranium seed germinates erratically, so don't be in too much of a hurry to assume the seed isn't viable if it takes a long time to produce results.

Seed of alpine species may respond well to a simulation of its native conditions by being stratified – sown in pots of free-draining compost and then exposed to the elements during the winter. An artificial approximation can be reached by storing the seed in the refrigerator for a few weeks before sowing it.

The basic method I use to sow seed is to al-most fill small pots or containers with a general purpose compost. Depending on the texture, this may well benefit from the addition of a little vermiculite or fine grit to open it up. Sow the seed on the surface, cover with a layer of vermiculite, and stand the pot in water until the moisture rises up through the compost and can be seen to have reached the vermiculite. Stand on a hard surface until excess moisture has drained off, then place in a cold frame or under the staging in a cold greenhouse. Prick out into trays or small individual pots when the first true leaves have formed.

Recommended methods of propagation for individual varieties are included in the respective entries in the A-Z of Geraniums in Cultivation.

PROPAGATION OF GERANIUM CINEREUM AND SIMILAR SPECIES

by Allan Robinson

Some of the most delightful geraniums are the alpine, or montane species, but because of their small size and compact growth the method of propagating them differs from that of the large border varieties. Species such as *Geranium cinereum*, *G. argenteum* and the hybrid between them, *G. × lindavicum*, offer a limited amount of cutting material, but by taking cuttings at the right time and with careful preparation, success should be assured.

Cuttings root easily if taken early in the season, before the plant starts to make new growth. In the UK, February to April is a good guide, although the weather is a contributing factor. A cold frame or greenhouse is essential, preferably with a soil-warming cable. An important part of the rooting process is placing the cuttings into a warm environment which produces rapid growth. It is too late to take cuttings when the plant commences vigorous growth outside as this reduces the strike rate.

Plastic pots are the best containers to use, as terracotta greatly reduces success. Pots approximately 5in (13cm) deep are the most suitable. Crushed grit is mounded at the base of the pot, the depth of the mound ¾in (2cm) at the edge, rising to 1½in (4cm) in the centre. A layer of compost is then added. A loam-based compost is best, with the addition of some limestone grit or sharp sand to improve drainage. Ground chalk is also useful as an additive as this helps to reduce fungal infection by increasing the pH level. Leave a space about 2–2½in (5–6cm) above the compost for the addition of sharp sand. Pile sand high over the pot rim, tap firmly about twenty times, level it off, and the pot is then ready for use. It is essential that deep pots are used, which automatically improves the drainage, and combined with the mounded grit, results in a perfectly drained container.

G. *sinense*

G. *incanum*
var. *multifidum*

G. 'Joy'

G. *traversii* var. *elegans*

G. *phaeum* 'Samobor' (leaf)

G. *pratense* forma *albiflorum*

Before the plant starts to make new growth in the spring, take cuttings 2-2½in (5-6cm) long — these should have a woody base. Remove all foliage from the cutting except for the emerging leaf, which is not usually mature. Make a cut 1½-2in (4-5cm) below the emerging leaf. This cut should slant from one side to another, opening up the vascular system and forming an artificial 'heel' which is approximately ½-¾in (1.5-2cm) long. A species such as *Geranium argenteum* may only produce short cuttings, in which case use the longest material possible.

If large numbers of cuttings are required, all top growth from the plant can be removed, leaving just a stump. This will regenerate into a fresh plant within a few months, and is an ideal way of renovating an old plant.

Root cuttings are another method of propagation for this group of geraniums. Many types of erodium also respond well to this treatment. If material from the open ground is to be used, the plant has to be lifted. Strong, healthy roots should be selected — avoid thin or weak ones. Cut the root into sections 1½-2in (4-5cm) long, cutting straight across the root on the top cut, but using a slanting cut on the lower one. This enables correct re-alignment in the case of accidental disturbance. The root cuttings are then inserted into exactly the same type of cutting container as mentioned above, leaving only the top ⅛in (3mm) exposed. Water them daily and give good light without allowing the exposed root to dry out. After two to three weeks have elapsed, a green 'ring' will appear on the top of the root cutting: this is a very good sign, as leaf growth will soon follow.

The other method is for pot-grown material, using the 'sand bed' technique widely used by nurseries in the past. For the best results, plants should be grown on a bed of sand 4-6in (10-15cm) deep for most of the preceding summer. The following spring, lift the pot slightly at one side, slide in the sharpest, most flexible knife you have, cut through all the roots and remove the pot. Good light and careful watering are essential, as the sand must not be allowed to dry out completely. During inclement weather, glass cloches may be used to protect the cuttings and also prevent waterlogging. Remove glass lights whenever the weather allows.

The best tool for taking both types of cuttings is the ordinary razor blade. The reason for this is that because of its thinness it destroys far fewer cells on its journey through the stem or root than other blades. However, they must be new blades — those discarded after domestic use are no good at all, for even a new blade becomes dull fairly quickly. Where top cuttings have been taken, the use of some hormone rooting powder is desirable, as the fungicide incorporated in this helps to prevent damping-off. Always make sure your rooting powder is fresh. It is advisable to purchase this from an outlet with a very quick turnover, as this product degenerates quickly and only has a very short shelf-life.

Aftercare is important to make sure that the cutting grows on steadily until it is sufficiently well rooted and sturdy to plant out.

5

HISTORICAL
AND HERBAL

Exploring the stages by which geraniums have been introduced into cultivation from the wild, and from overseas, is an absorbing pastime. Most of the early evidence comes from documents relating to the great herbalists of the sixteenth and seventeenth centuries, who grew geraniums in their physic gardens for academic study and possible use in medicine. These were the first varieties which were available for planting in ordinary gardens for purely decorative effect. As interest grew, plant collectors sought out new varieties, and chance hybrids were seized upon to increase the range. Garden writers devoted more space to them, raising awareness and creating demand for ever more species and hybrids which, however, have mainly stemmed from a few familiar geraniums which are truly native, and others which are very long established.

In *The Concise British Flora in Colour* (1965) by the Reverend William Keble Martin, sixteen species of geraniums are listed as growing wild in the British Isles. Twelve of these are described in the British Natives section of the A-Z list (Chapter 11). Nine of the twelve are rather weedy, but there are three species which are acceptable as good garden plants, namely *Geranium pratense*, *G. sanguineum* and *G. sylvaticum*. Named varieties which have been derived from them, and are well known in the garden, are detailed in the main part of the A-Z list. The remaining four species are noted by Keble Martin as 'Not native – alien'. This indicates that they were introduced from other parts of Europe so long ago that they have become accepted as honorary natives through having

escaped into the wild and flourished there. These four are *Geranium endressii*, *G. nodosum*, *G. phaeum* and *G. versicolor*.

Geranium phaeum was the first to be introduced, before the end of the sixteenth century, followed by *G. versicolor* (then called *G. striatum*) in 1629 from Italy, *G. nodosum* from southern Europe in 1633, and *G. endressii* from the Pyrenees in the early nineteenth century. The herbalist and botanist John Gerard (1545–1612) grew the native species *G. pratense* and *G. sanguineum* in his garden, as well as *G. phaeum* and *G. tuberosum*, which had been introduced from Italy in 1596. His contemporary John Parkinson (1567–1650) also grew these, plus *G. striatum* (*G. versicolor*). *Geranium macrorrhizum* came in from Italy in 1596, and there are records of it being grown in the Oxford Botanic Garden in 1658.

Geranium sanguineum was reported as growing wild on Ingleborough in Yorkshire in 1666, its favourite native habitats being on limestone or sand. It was cultivated in physic gardens for its use as a wound-healing herb, which is thought to be the reason for its epithet of 'bloody cranesbill' rather than its colour. By 1732 there are reports of its delightful variety *G.s.* var. *lancastriense* (now *G.s.* var. *striatum*) growing in a botanic garden in Eltham.

It can only be guessed that some of the native species were grown in ordinary gardens. The cottage garden tended to have space only for purely practical plants – useful for food, cleaning or medicine. There is scanty evidence that geraniums fit into these categories to any great degree. But such early introductions as

Geranium phaeum and *G. versicolor*, which are notorious colonisers, may well have escaped quite quickly into the wild from the plantsmen's gardens, and then been brought into general cultivation as cottage gardens progressed to being more decorative.

A rough indication as to whether plants were well established and widely appreciated for their practical value can be gauged from whether they feature in folklore, and have accumulated a wide variety of local nicknames. *Geranium pratense* for example has very few of these common names, although 'Blue Basins' is reasonably popular. It is sometimes included in present day herb gardens for the sake of its decorative appearance and a reputed use of its flowers for dyeing.

Geranium phaeum is well known as 'Dusky Cranesbill' or 'Mourning Widow' from the sombre colour of its flowers, and *G. versicolor* as 'Queen Anne's Needlework' or 'Painted Lady' from its intricate veining. *G. maculatum*, introduced from North America in 1732, was used as an astringent and tonic, useful for treating internal bleeding and chronic dysentery. The British native annual *G. dissectum* was found to have very similar properties.

However, the two which are deeply entrenched in folklore and the old herbals are both native annuals which are now generally disregarded as garden plants. They are *Geranium molle*, Soft Cranesbill, and *G. robertianum*, Herb Robert.

G. molle is also known as Dove's Foot Cranesbill, and was extolled by John Gerard for its medicinal properties. He then went on to confuse the issue by quoting its botanical name as *G. columbinum* which is quite a different species. His description however, definitely fits that of *G. molle*, which he recommended highly for the treatment of ruptures.

> The herbe and roots dried, beaten into most fine powder, and given halfe a spoonfull fasting, and the like quantity to bedwards in red wine, or old claret, for the space of one and twenty daies together, cure miraculously ruptures or burstings, as my selfe have often proved, whereby I have gotten crownes and credit.

He goes on to give a rather revolting variation on this recipe, for curing ruptures 'in aged persons' which involves adding a powder made from nine oven-dried slugs.

It is *Geranium robertianum* which has the widest coverage, the most comprehensive list of medicinal uses, and the most interesting array of regional nicknames – Geoffrey Grigson in *The Englishman's Flora* lists 111. Some of these are frivolous and funny, such as 'baby's pinafore' and 'chatterboxes' but others have a decidedly morbid or sinister sound, such as 'adder's tongue', 'bloodwort' and 'death come quickly'. Its uses seemed to span the whole range of human suffering, from toothache and nosebleed to gout and afflictions of a more delicate nature.

As a garden plant, Herb Robert has its attractions, but needs a sharp eye kept on it to thwart a complete takeover bid. If grown in good garden soil, it makes a lusty plant which can then mask and overwhelm any 'little treasure' of a weaker constitution. There is a blush-pink form which makes a change, and both sorts have leaves which colour brilliantly in winter. However the pure white-flowered variety *Geranium r.* 'Celtic White' is extremely neat and tidy, a miniature version with fresh green, finely cut leaves, almost parsley-like. It seeds around mildly but not usually enough to be a threat.

6
PEOPLE
AND THEIR PLANTS

Like all the best garden plants, geraniums have the ability to make people enthuse about them and to communicate that enthusiasm to others. There are also plantsmen and explorers who delight in searching out previously unknown varieties or in creating improved versions of those that already exist.

SOME ENTHUSIASTS

William Robinson in his book *The Wild Garden* (1870) wrote about geraniums in his campaign to persuade people to grow more native plants and to grow them in more informal and natural ways, rather than conforming to the craze for carpet bedding which was then at its height. By 1883, however, when he wrote *The English Flower Garden*, Robinson was going into more detail about imported varieties such as *G. armenum* (now *G. psilostemon*) and *G. ibericum*, and advocating their use in borders, beds and shrubberies.

E.A. Bowles (1865–1954) did a great deal of plant collecting in Europe. Being a martyr to hay fever he was obliged to spend the summertime in the rarefied atmosphere of the Alps, where he collected and sent home enormous consignments of plants, including many varieties of geranium, which were added to his collection at Myddelton House, Enfield. He wrote delightfully about them in *My Garden in Summer* (1914) and a series of articles in *The Garden* magazine in 1921. His obvious love of geraniums and his minutely detailed observations about them, must have brought them to the attention of many gardeners for the first time. He was fascinated by the intricate veining in many of the flowers, particularly those of *G. pratense* and *G. platypetalum*. He noted their relative opacity or transparency and the way this affected the colour and appearance of the flowers. Through his plant hunting expeditions he became acquainted with Reginald Farrer, amongst whose discoveries was the geranium which now bears his name, *G. farreri*.

Bowles was also a great friend of two other notable plantsmen of the time, who lived quite near each other in Wales. **A.T. Johnson** (1873–1956) and **E.C. Buxton** (1838–1925) have both been immortalised by having geraniums named after them – *G.* × *oxonianum* 'A.T. Johnson', *G.* 'Johnson's Blue' and *G. wallichianum* 'Buxton's Variety'. Mr Johnson wrote enthusiastically in several books, including *A Garden in Wales* and *A Woodland Garden*, about the wide range of geraniums he grew. He also wrote a booklet *Labour Saving Plants* commending their virtues in low-maintenance gardening.

Walter Ingwersen collected a number of geraniums in the wild, which in due course became available through his nursery. As well as the most widely grown form of *G. macrorrhizum* – *G.m.* 'Ingwersen's Variety' – he also discovered *G.m. album*, *G. dalmaticum* and *G. renardii*, the latter of which is sometimes known as *G.r.* 'Walter Ingwersen'. It is an interesting point of continuity that Ingwersen's Birch Farm Nursery is situated on part of William Robinson's old estate at Gravetye in West Sussex, and has produced *G. himalayense* 'Gravetye' as well as *G.h.* 'Birch Double' (*G.h.* 'Plenum').

G. x *oxonianum* 'A. T. Johnson' is one of the longest established of the named varieties. The well-shaped leaves and extended season of silvery-pink flowers make it a reliable choice for ground cover or underplanting shrubs

Arthur Johnson's friend E. C. Buxton is remembered in this distinctive and very popular form of *G. wallichianum*. The true blue flowers of *G.w.* 'Buxton's Variety' are carried on trailing stems from late summer right through to the frosts, when the mottled leaves go red

Everything about this hybrid of G. *psilostemon* – smaller scale, softer colour – makes *G.p.* 'Bressingham Flair' much easier to place in the garden

Margery Fish was converted to the geranium cause by E.A. Bowles. She enjoyed visiting his garden and admired the way he used geraniums in mixed plantings, especially in shade. Over the years she acquired many new varieties, and in her books she related how she moved them around until she found just the right spot for them. She also endowed them with personalities, saying of G. *endressii's* versatility, 'It never seems out of place. Put it among the aristocrats and it is as dignified as they are, let it romp in a cottage garden and it becomes a simple maid in a print dress'.

Undoubtedly the plantsman of today who has had the greatest influence on the plant-loving public is **Graham Stuart Thomas.** When he was director of Sunningdale Nurseries he transformed the nursery catalogue into literature with *The Modern Florilegium*, including enthusiastic and erudite descriptions of a number of hardy geraniums. This was later expanded into his indispensable book *Perennial Garden Plants* (1976). There is also a comprehensive coverage of cranesbills in his *Plants for Ground Cover* (1970).

But no full-length work on the subject had been published until *Hardy Geraniums* by **Peter F. Yeo** came out in 1985. This described all the varieties available at the time in great technical detail with a tremendous amount of background information.

Contemporary plant collectors who have enriched our gardens include **Roy Lancaster**, who has introduced many new species such as *Geranium gracile* from north-eastern Turkey, and G. *kishtvariense* from Kashmir. **Bill Baker** brought back the definitive pink form of G. *sylvaticum* from the Swiss Alps, which is now known as G. *sylvaticum* 'Baker's Pink', and G. *ibericum* subsp. *jubatum* from north-eastern Turkey. **Alan Bloom** of Bloom's Nurseries at Bressingham in Norfolk has created a number of popular hybrids, including G. *cinereum* 'Ballerina', G. *cinereum* 'Lawrence Flatman', G. *sylvaticum* 'Mayflower' and G. 'Bressingham Flair'. The latest introduction has been named G. *sanguineum* 'Alan Bloom' in honour of his eighty-fifth birthday.

GERANIUMS COLLECTED IN THE WILD

by Roy Lancaster

I suppose the very first wild geranium I ever collected was our native *Geranium sanguineum* which I found on the limestone paving above Silverdale in north Lancashire. It grew there in abundance and the seedling I selected, with flowers darker than the rest, was destined for a small rock garden I had recently constructed in the garden of my childhood home in Bolton. That was almost forty years and a lot of geraniums ago. I collected this species again in 1977, this time growing on a stony hillside in Anatolia, north-eastern Turkey; and for many years it grew on the screes in the Sir Harold Hillier Gardens and Arboretum in Hampshire. For all I know it is still there.

My principal memory of Turkish geraniums however, relates to the woods and meadows I visited in the Pontic Alps above Trabzon, an area with a rich flora, and a garden-lover's delight. It was here that I collected *Geranium gracile* (L.79). Gracile is a good name, for this is a species of slender erect growth with quietly attractive foliage and pink funnel-shaped flowers that look you in the eye. Scattered plants of it were growing in light woodland on a steep escarpment beneath the famous Sumela Monastery which at the time of our visit was in a depressing state. My friend Bill Baker was with me, and he also collected this species, as well as the more obvious *G. psilostemon* which we saw later the same day. Today, *G. gracile* grows in my garden in a mixed perennial shrub border where it enjoys shelter and dappled shade.

Bill and I also collected *Geranium ibericum* that day from the same valley where it grew on a rough grassy slope in full sun. I still have my plant (L.70) which is attractive without being a scene stealer. Far better is a collection I made of *G. platypetalum* in the Caucasus in 1979. I was climbing up a valley near the Klukorsky Pass above Sochumi (dangerous territory now) when I found the geranium growing with *Veronica peduncularis* on the edge of a snow patch. Some

of the geraniums were partially covered by the melting snow, and one seedling (L.336) was enough to establish this species in my garden.

Here it has flourished to such an extent that it regularly seeds around, the resultant seedlings seemingly identical with the mother plant. It is a charming plant of relatively compact habit, forming a low mound of softly downy, rounded leaves with up to nine lobes, which are in turn lobed. It is the flowers, however, that give this plant class. The broad petals overlap, giving the flower a neatly rounded appearance. In colour I suppose it is blue-violet, though nearer blue than violet, and I would not be without it.

Several knowledgeable visitors to my garden have commented on this plant in flower. When, some years ago, I had a visit from Dr Hans Simon, whose nursery at Markthiedenfeld is a must for plant enthusiasts, I determined to show my geranium to him. Any thoughts I had of leading him to the plant gradually were immediately dashed when, stepping out of his car in my drive, he spotted it in full flower in the nearby border. He was impressed, and, convinced that it was an improvement on the species as normally grown in cultivation, in Germany certainly, he persuaded me to give it a cultivar name, hence 'Georgia Blue'. I also named the clone of *Veronica peduncularis* I collected 'Georgia Blue', but this the International Code of Nomenclature for Cultivated Plants allows me to do, given that the recipients belong to different genera.

One of my most exciting discoveries involving geraniums occurred in Kashmir in 1978 where, above Gulmarg north of the capital Srinagar, I found several species growing on the margins of forest in the mountains. One of these, *Geranium wallichianum*, I did not collect, as the flowers were of no particular merit. I did however collect another geranium which, though I was not to know it at the time, would cause quite a stir.

It was a rather straggling plant as I saw it in the field, with sharply toothed, three- to five-lobed

G. kishtvariense, with rich purple flowers, comes from Kashmir
and was introduced into cultivation by Roy Lancaster

leaves, and rich purple flowers, each petal with a white V-shaped basal marking and dark venation. It appeared to possess a creeping rootstock as its flowers popped up in several places in the herbage. I managed to detach a rooted piece (L.159) which I wrapped in damp moss and brought home in my pocket. I also collected – without realising it – a plant of the same species (L.177) from a rough pasture above Gulmarg and just below the plateau called Khillanmarg.

Some time after my return I gave material of this geranium to Peter Yeo, who grew it on at the University of Cambridge Botanic Garden. One day a year or so later, I had a phone call from Peter, telling me that my plant which he had been comparing first with *Geranium rectum* and then with *G. rubifolium* was a distinct species of *G. kishtvariense* and furthermore that it was probably the first introduction to cultivation. The story concerning the history of this species and its naming is told in Dr Yeo's *Hardy Geraniums* (1985) and makes fascinating reading. Now *G. kishtvariense* is available from a number of nurseries, in Britain certainly, and seems to have been accepted as a worthwhile plant.

From the open slopes above Gulmarg I also collected a geranium (L.158) which was referred to by Peter Yeo over the years first as *Geranium* sp. then progressively as *G. pratense* Kashmir form, *G.* 'Kashmir Purple' and finally *G. clarkei* 'Kashmir Purple'. It had been collected by others before me, of course, but its identity had taxed a lot of minds before Dr Yeo's 'final' solution. It has a far-creeping rootstock and forms extensive colonies in its native pastures, while in gardens it can overrun less robust perennials that grow in its path. With its finely divided, fragile-looking leaves and beautiful purple-violet flowers on slender stalks, this is a distinct and lovely cranesbill. I never understood how it could be linked to *G. pratense*.

Sooner or later I was bound to get around to Chinese geraniums, and here again I have been fortunate in having seen some of the most interesting species. In 1984 for instance I visited the Changbai Shan region of China's Jilin pro-vince in the north-east, on the border with North Korea. The wooded slopes of these mountains are well endowed with perennials of many kinds, and it is here that I encountered *Geranium eriostemon* var. *reinii*, identified for me by Peter Yeo.

There it enjoys light woodland shade and is commonly found in glades as well as by road-sides and trails. I collected two seedlings, only one of which (L.1261) now seems to be in cultivation. A plant in my garden grows in the shade of a magnolia in a rather dry sandy border and though its pale violet-blue flowers are not in the front rank, its handsome leaf pile in autumn usually gives rich orange and red tints.

A photograph of this plant in the wild appears in my book *Travels in China*, whilst in the same publication appears a photograph of *Geranium yunnanense*, a species introduced to cultivation for the first time in 1981 by the Sino-British Expedition to Yunnan. We found the latter growing in a wooded ravine in the mountains above Huadianba at the northern end of the Cangshan, a range of mountains better known, to fans of George Forrest certainly, as the Tali range. It was first cultivated at the Royal Botanic Garden, Edinburgh, and my present plant (SBEC 962) came from there. A clump-forming perennial, it has nodding rose-pink, bowl-shaped flowers with blackish anthers carried above the attractive piles of three- to five-lobed leaves. I have seen this species thriving at Edinburgh but I have twice lost it in my own garden, whether due to winter wet or cold I cannot be sure. In the warmer south of England it might pay to plant it in a sheltered, well-drained position open to the sky but not to the undiluted summer sun.

In 1990 a plant flowered for the first time in my garden since I collected it as seed in 1986 (L.1681). It had small pinkish-lilac nodding flowers with reflexed petals not unlike those of *Geranium phaeum*. The only thing was, I had collected the seed at 11,150ft (3,400m) on the eastern flank of the Yulongshan or Jade Dragon Mountains in north-west Yunnan. Checking it out in Peter Yeo's book, it appeared to agree with the description of *G. delavayi*, the opening

70

paragraph of which ended 'probably not in cultivation'. I checked again and I became more certain than ever of its identity. I sent a specimen to Peter, who initially would not commit himself. Later however, having seen living plants at Washfield Nursery in Kent, he agreed that *G. delavayi* it most certainly was. What the origin of the Washfield stock is, I do not know, but it is possible it may be a result of seed collected in the Yulongshan by the RHS-Kew expedition in 1987.

In the past, *G. delavayi* has been confused with the closely related *G. sinense* which, as usually seen, has blackish-crimson flowers. Indeed, according to Yeo, both A.T. Johnson and Walter Ingwersen grew and praised *G. sinense* believing it to be *G. delavayi*. The growth and growing requirements of the two are very similar. The only differences botanically, Yeo writes, are found in leaf and flower characters, requiring close examination; for example, flowers with one nectary forming a ring round the flower in *G. sinense*, and with five nectaries in *G. delavayi*.

One of my favourite alpine geraniums is *Geranium pylzowianum* which I have admired ever since I first met with it on a northern rock garden in the 1950s. In 1981 I saw this delightful little creeping species by the side of a track in the Pa La river valley west of Minya Konka in west Sichuan. I did not collect it then, but my companion Alan Leslie did. In 1986 I found it again, growing on the stony slopes of Zheg Shan (Partridge Mountain) in north-west Sichuan, west of Songpan. It was September, and although the plant had finished flowering, seed was plentiful

and a pinch of this (L.1550) was all I needed to establish it with me. Now it occupies over 12in (30cm) square of sandy ground in one of my mixed beds. Its long creeping rhizomes with tiny tubers run in every direction, sending up small, slender-stalked, deeply lobed leaves and deep rose-pink flowers – surprisingly large for the size of the plant. It loves full sun and a free-draining soil and seems one of the easiest of the alpine species to establish.

As always, space has run out and I have still more geraniums to tell you about. However, in the hope that it will be of use to those who grow any of my collections, I shall end this brief account with a list of those geraniums I have introduced or had a hand in introducing during the last twenty years or so.

G. clarkei 'Kashmir Purple'	L.158
G. delavayi	L.1681
G. eriostemon var. *reinii*	L.1243 and L.1261
G. gracile	L.79
G. hispidissimum	L.1685 A
G. ibericum	L.70
G. kishtvariense	L.159 and L.177
G. oreganum	L.1881
G. platypetalum 'Georgia Blue'	L.336
G. polyanthes	B,L and M.29
G. pylzowianum	L.1550
G. sanguineum	L.54
G. stapfianum	L.916
G. strigosum	L.1658 B
G. yunnanense	SBEC 962
G. sp.	L.942
G. sp.	L.1669

IN SEARCH OF GERANIUMS

by Bill Baker

There is no greater thrill than finding for the first time in the wild some special plant, and geraniums come into this category. Even if you already grow the geranium in your garden, it is

like meeting an old friend, and almost as exciting.

Not long after the last war our holidays were spent walking in Austria, sleeping in the mountain huts, and so I developed a keen interest in

G. clarkei 'Kashmir Purple'

G. *himalayense* 'Plenum'

G. *robustum*

G. *pratense* 'Plenum Violaceum'

G. *pratense* 'Plenum Caeruleum'

G. *kishtvariense*

G. 'Salome'

G. *lambertii*

72

This fine pink form of G. *sylvaticum* was discovered in Switzerland by Bill Baker, and is now known as G.s. 'Baker's Pink'

alpine plants. This led me to joining the Alpine Garden Society and going on various tours to the Dolomites, northern Italy and Switzerland, led by Gerard Parker, a friend of E.A. Bowles. It taught me a great deal about plants, and here my interest in geraniums began.

From these early travels I came home with *Geranium rivulare*. the typical form of *G. sylvaticum*, and a large-flowered *G. phaeum* var. *lividum*. This latter has produced a very attractive pale lilac seedling which Axletree Nursery has named 'Joan Baker' after my wife.

On a more recent visit to Switzerland, a very fine pink form of *Geranium sylvaticum* was the highlight, and is mentioned in *Hardy Geraniums* by Peter Yeo (1985). I had intended calling it 'Wengen' but this proved to be an unpopular name, and it is now in several nurseries as *G.s.* 'Baker's Pink'.

On the same holiday I noticed one white *Geranium pyrenaicum* growing in a population of normal coloured ones. This has proved to be more than successful, seeding happily all over my garden. However, unwanted plants are easily pulled up, and the foliage is extremely fragrant.

Then on a visit to the Atlas mountains I found *Geranium malviflorum* growing on a rocky bank. In those days it had the appropriate name of *G. atlanticum*. It behaves like many plants from the Mediterranean, resting in the summer then producing leaves in the autumn and flowering very early. It is not just confined to Morocco, because I found a pinkish-blue form in southern Spain which flowers a fortnight later. Actually *G. malviflorum* is not the earliest geranium to flower with me, but another tuberous one, *G. libani*, collected in the Lebanon, before the troubles, by old friends Mollie and Herbert Crook.

The Peloponnese appropriately produced *Geranium peloponnesiacum*, a blue flower with darker veins, and leaves similar in texture to *G. renardii*. It was growing in open woodland, and does well in the garden. On Mount Chelmos in a very different habitat amidst snow, and with *Tulipa australe* and *Crocus sieberi* forma *tricolor* for company, was a geranium only 5in (13cm) high, like a miniature malviflorum. This proved to be *G. macrostylum*, and has been on my rock garden for over thirty years.

Many years later I visited northern Greece, concentrating on the Pindus mountains, where I was snowed up in a mountain hut with Roy Lancaster. Here *Geranium subcaulescens* was growing, its bright red colour making it easy to see, and nearby grew a dwarf form of *G. macrorrhizum*, which maintains its dwarf form in cultivation.

That Greek trip also resulted in *Geranium brutium*, which just appeared, having come in the soil with another plant. It behaves as a self-sowing annual, which seems to have vanished from my garden at the moment, unfortunately, but may well pop up again one day. The more usual form of *G. macrorrhizum* was seen in the woods of the Maritime Alps, a very rewarding place for wild geraniums. There I found a form of *G. nodosum* with a dark centre and almost white edges to its pink petals – a very fine plant. *G. sanguineum* was plentiful, looking far less magenta than those at home.

Turkey, mostly the north-east area, was excellent for geraniums; *G. ibericum* and *G.*

psilostemon being good for the border, and G. *gracile* and G. *asphodeloides* for the wild garden.

My garden is cold and wet, so sun-lovers suffer, but one geranium thrives and has produced a very worthy hybrid. The original plant was *Geranium palustre* and it was growing in a damp meadow with *Euphorbia palustre*, in the Caucasus. The hybrid I call 'Palustre Plus', because it is better than the type and has a few extra chromosomes from something else. I thought the other parent was G. *gracile* but Dr Yeo suspects G. *sylvaticum*. From the same part of the world came a brown G. *phaeum*, but it may well be G. *reflexum*. All forms of G. *phaeum* are welcome, whether in white, blue or pink, besides the normal black, and all grow in dense shade. High in the mountains in Russia, I realised I was walking on the lovely leaves of G. *renardii*, but not a flower was to be seen.

Then in Central Asia on a hot dry hillside, I was shown *Geranium charlesii*. It is very much like the widespread G. *tuberosum* which I've seen in Armenia and Cyprus. I was not able to collect G. *charlesii* but G. *collinum*, and a blue-flowered geranium, near-pratense, made it safely home. The Russians confiscated one lot of plants, but two from previous years got by.

In north-western America my only discovery was *Geranium viscosissimum*. It was growing in hot dry sagebrush country, so it is short-lived in my garden. New England however was the home of G. *maculatum* and it was growing by the thousand on Cape Cod. A long search resulted in finding one with larger and deeper pink flowers, and this is a very permanent plant.

My last plant hunting trip was to China, and most successful, with primulas, paeonies, iris, roscoeas and even a new daphne, but alas of geraniums only the small-flowered G. *thunbergii* – useful in herbal medicine, but of no use in the garden.

In future my search for wild geraniums will have to be in the seed lists and catalogues of specialist societies. It will be far less trouble, definitely less expensive and perhaps just as rewarding, if not quite so exciting.

ALAN BREMNER
AND THE ORKNEY HYBRIDS

Alan Bremner is a farmer on Orkney, who is a very enthusiastic member of the Hardy Plant Society's Hardy Geranium Group. In 1988 he carried out an interesting survey of the geraniums being grown in Orkney gardens, reporting on some sixty-four varieties, a surprising number of which did well under difficult conditions, though seed was not always readily produced.

Being so isolated from the mainland and therefore unable to take part in group meetings, he has concentrated for some years on an intensive programme of geranium hybridisation. He was initially inspired by *Hardy Geraniums* by Peter Yeo (1985) which gave details of chromosome numbers in the various geranium species.

Although this is only one of the factors which determines the successful outcome of deliberate hybridisation, a knowledge of chromosome numbers is a vital first step towards increasing the chances of producing a viable and fertile hybrid.

Dr Yeo listed the known hybrids up to that date and then detailed the method for making controlled crossings, as opposed to growing plants close together and letting nature take its course. Alan then embarked on an intensive programme of controlled pollination of geraniums, which has produced a wide range of hybrids, some of them from unlikely pairings.

The whole process is necessarily labour intensive and long term, as the resulting seedlings

74

have to be grown on for some time before settling down and showing their individuality. It is also necessary to grow them on to assess their garden worthiness. Much of this trialling has been carried out by David Hibberd at Axletree Nursery in East Sussex. Both David Hibberd and Alan Bremner have written a number of progress reports in the newsletters of the HPS Hardy Geranium Group, and the Geraniaceae Group of the British Pelargonium and Geranium Society, where more detailed treatment of the observations can be found.

As well as creating new and distinctive hybrids, the aim was to re-create existing ones which were difficult to find. It was also hoped to fill some gaps in the present range of hardy geraniums, for example a dwarf, blue-flowered geranium suitable for the rock garden would fill a long-felt want. There was also great interest in seeing which apparently dissimilar species might initially produce viable seed, and then a seedling with the best features of both parents but a personality of its own.

In some hybrids the characteristics of one parent are more dominant and tend to mask the contribution of the other. Hybrids produced by crossing *Geranium endressii*, *G.* × *oxonianum*, *G. pratense* and *G. collinum* with *G. psilostemon*, all produced tall plants with flowers most resembling those of *G. psilostemon*, although the colour of the flowers varied and sometimes the petals were separated. However, using the same cross that produced *Geranium* 'Ann Folkard' (*G. procurrens* × *G. psilostemon*) the relation to *G. procurrens* was very evident.

THE PROCEDURE

Potting up The routine starts in late winter or early spring, when the plants to be used for hybridising can be potted up, so that before reaching flowering stage they can be brought into the greenhouse or otherwise isolated. They are potted up in a free-draining compost with a slow-release fertiliser incorporated. One plant which does not take happily to being potted up is *Geranium lambertii*, as it then produces plenty of leaves but very few flowers. Growing plants under cover often results in extra vigorous but soft growth, so that support is necessary. For example, *G. traversii* and *G. procurrens* are difficult because they make such a lot of growth anyway. *G. traversii* can spread to cover 39in (100cm) in a season. If trailing growth is resting on the rim of a pot, the pressure can result in a restriction of the flow of nutrients and water along that stem, causing a check to development. In one particular incident, *G. procurrens* was carefully enclosed in a tall cylinder of wire netting which it quickly outgrew, so the pot had to be raised up on progressively taller bases.

Most geranium flowers open in early to mid-morning; the most likely ones can be assessed from the state of the buds on the previous evening, and an advance selection made of those to be used for cross-pollination. When the flowers open, the anthers will soon burst and release the pollen. The ten anthers open in two stages, five at a time. Large-flowered species are geared to cross-pollination, so the anthers (male) and the stigma (female) are ready in succession, but the small-flowered species, and the annuals, are self-pollinated, so the whole process happens more or less simultaneously.

Emasculation The petals, and the stamens which bear the anthers, are removed with fine-pointed tweezers. The remainder of the flower now has to be enclosed to prevent the stigma from being accidentally fertilised from any other source. Alan has found that the most effective covers are small bags made from glassine, a kind of glazed translucent paper which is more durable than ordinary paper and can be written on, although one visitor to his greenhouse wanted to know why all the plants were covered with teabags! These bags are available from stationer's shops, listed as 'showcase packets'. The stigma is ready for fertilisation when it branches into five. The flowers selected as pollen parents can be bagged to prevent casual contamination by insects. Alternatively, flowers can be picked from the garden before opening, and kept fresh by standing in a small amount of water, isolated from insects.

Pollination Each stamen is picked up with tweezers and the pollen from the anther is carefully stroked on to the stigma. The flower is then re-covered with the glassine bag, which is marked with the name of the pollen parent and the date. Frequent inspection is required to check if the pollination has been successful. If it has, the rostrum or beak (the seed pod) will soon start to develop. If it has not been successful, the flower will wither. The time taken from pollination to seed harvest is variable, but is usually about a month.

Seed Collection The glassine bag prevents random dispersal of the seed. This can be collected as soon as the beak (seed pod) turns brown, when the whole flowerhead can be transferred to a paper bag for final ripening, or left on the plant till fully ripe. The seed can then be stored in a cool, dry cupboard, ready for sowing in the usual way.

Growing On Hybrid seedlings often have yellow foliage, and further growth is delayed and weakened by this lack of chlorophyll, which means they must be kept away from strong sunlight. They are also more prone to fungal disease. The length of time taken to reach flowering size is very variable. Some achieve this in their first season, particularly hybrids of *Geranium sessiliflorum* and *G. traversii*, but larger varieties such as hybrids of *G. pratense* will usually need a second season to reach this stage. One of the frustrating factors is that sometimes the first cross in the breeding programme is successful, but the resulting hybrid is sterile, so that it cannot be used for the next stage in the programme.

SUMMING UP

Over six years, Alan has made 314 interspecific crosses (between two different species) and thirty-six crosses of species with hybrids. Sixty-two viable hybrids have been produced, of which fifty were interspecific, and the other twelve from species crossed with hybrids.

One of the most difficult things, requiring the judgement of Solomon, is to sort out the most promising seedlings from each batch, which can then be grown on to assess their long-term value. Several varieties which have already been proved garden-worthy have been named, and introduced commercially.

The ideal weather conditions during the various stages of the operation would be warm and dry, quite different from the usual cool and damp climate in Orkney! Obviously the whole procedure needs a great deal of patience and skill. Alan says it is not as time-consuming as it might appear on paper – once the routine is established it becomes a matter of course. It can be relaxing and rewarding in spite of various frustrations and setbacks. In fact, Alan warns that it may become addictive! There is always the possibility of a miracle within the next batch of seed, and always new goals to strive for.

NEW HYBRIDS
RAISED BY ALAN BREMNER

G. 'Anne Thomson' (*G. procurrens* × *G. psilostemon*) has the same parentage as *G.* 'Ann Folkard' and identical flowers, though more compact in habit, 22in (56cm) high, with a spread of 36in (91cm). The young leaves are less gold-tinged than those of 'Ann Folkard' and the growth not so straggly towards the end of the season.

G. 'Black Ice' (*G. traversii* × *G. sessiliflorum* ssp. *novaezelandii* 'Nigricans') forms a mound of dark bronze foliage, spreading to 40in (100cm) or more when established. Small, white, occasionally pale pink flowers are produced over a long period, contrasting effectively with the leaves. G. 'Black Ice' is suitable for the large rock garden, trailing over rocks or a wall where it has plenty of room to develop.

G. 'Chantilly' (*G. renardii* × *G. gracile*) is a prettily dainty geranium 18in (45cm) in height, somewhat similar to *G. gracile* but more compact in habit. In appearance the pale green leaves are midway between the parents. Slightly uptilted, lavender-pink flowers 1¼in (3cm) are freely produced in summer, creating the illusion

One of Alan Bremner's hybrids, G. 'Joy' is named after Joy Jones and is proving to be an excellent garden plant for both flower and foliage interest

of a pink cloud. G. 'Chantilly' was introduced by Axletree Nursery.

G. 'Dilys' (G. *sanguineum* × G. *procurrens*) was named after Dilys Davies, a leading member of the HPS, and is intermediate in habit between the parents, but with leaves very similar to those of G. *sanguineum*. It forms a mound up to 9in (23cm) and spreads to about 36in (91cm). The flowers 1 ¼in (3cm) are a soft purple with deep purple veins. Like G. *procurrens* it has a long flowering season, from late summer to autumn. It was introduced by Axletree Nursery.

G. 'Joy' (G. *traversii* var. *elegans* × G. *lambertii*) was named after Joy Jones. My namesake forms neat mounds of almost evergreen marbled leaves. The bowl-shaped flowers 1 ¼in (3cm) are a soft pink with prominent darker veins produced over an exceptionally long season, from spring to autumn. 'Joy' seems to be hardy and makes an attractive plant for the rock garden or front of the border. Stem cuttings are easily rooted. Introduced by Axletree Nursery.

G. 'Nora Bremner' (G. *rubifolium* × G. *wallichianum* 'Buxton's Variety') was named after Alan's mother. It makes leafy clumps of about 18in (45cm) in spread. The flowers 1 ¼in (3cm) are a lovely soft violet-blue with a white eye. Widely separated, shallowly notched petals create a starry appearance. Propagation is difficult as the rootstock cannot be divided, and cuttings are not easy to root.

G. 'Pagoda' (G. *sinense* × G. *yunnanense*) is described as an upright plant, though somewhat lax in habit, growing to about 24in (61cm). Like both its parents it has mottled leaves and nodding flowers 1 ¼in (3cm). The petals are flat but curl back slightly with age, and this evocation of the roofs of oriental temples caused Alan to choose this particular name! The remarkable colour is one not found hitherto in the whole genus, a dark reddish-purple with a velvety texture. The plant has a rather loose habit which makes it a useful plant for the wild or woodland garden, requiring some shade in drier areas. Some seed is produced, which could result in even more interesting progeny. 'Pagoda' was introduced by Axletree Nursery.

G. 'Patricia' (*G. endressii* × *G. psilostemon*) was named after Patricia Doughty. It is a magnificent geranium growing to about 30in (76cm) and producing a canopy of very large leaves. The large flowers 1½in (4cm) which are bright magenta with a dark, star-shaped eye, continue over a long period from early to late summer, making it a useful border plant.

G. 'Philippe Vapelle' (*G. renardii* × *G. platypetalum*) was raised in recent years by Ivan Louette in Belgium, but the same cross was also made by Alan Bremner, resulting in a plant indistinguishable from 'Philippe Vapelle'. The Bremner clone is being distributed by Axletree Nursery under this name, as permitted under the rules of the International Code of Nomenclature of Cultivated Plants. It makes neat mounds 15in (38cm) in height and spread, with lovely softly hairy, blue-grey leaves. The large, bluish-purple flowers with strong dark veins and notched petals are freely produced over a long period.

G. 'Rebecca' (*G. traversii* var *elegans* × *G. cinereum* var. *subcaulescens*) was named after Elaine R. Bullard. This small cranesbill has silvery evergreen leaves mounding up to 6in (15cm). The freely produced flowers are similar to those of *G. traversii* var. *elegans* – mid-pink with darker veins. It should prove a desirable plant for the rock garden, scree or trough.

G. 'Sea Fire' (*G. sessiliflorum* 'Nigricans' × *G. × oxonianum*) is a low spreading plant 8in (20cm) and 18in (45cm) wide. The evergreen leaves are less bronze-tinted than those of *G.* 'Sea Pink' but the flowers are more strongly coloured, bright red-pink with a pale eye, from early summer to early autumn. Introduced by Axletree Nursery, this is a plant suitable for the rock garden or front of the border.

The hybrid G. 'Philippe Vapelle' combines clear evidence of both parents – the flowers are reminiscent of *G. platypetalum*, and the leaves of *G. renardii* – resulting in a plant that has its own attractive individuality

G. 'Sea Pink' (*G. sessiliflorum* 'Nigricans' × *G. × oxonianum* has the same habit as *G.* 'Sea Fire' but the leaves are bronze-tinted and the flowers are pink with a pale centre. This geranium was introduced by Charterhouse Nursery.

G. 'Sea Spray' (*G. traversii* var. *elegans* × *G. sessiliflorum* 'Nigricans') forms mounds of bronze-tinted leaves with a spread of 40in (100cm) when established. The flowers vary from very pale pink to almost white and are produced continuously throughout the growing season. It was introduced by Cally Gardens.

At the time of writing, a number of these hybrids have been introduced, by the nurseries quoted. It is hoped that by the time this book is in print the other hybrids will also be commercially available.

7

THE NATIONAL COLLECTIONS

The National Council for the Conservation of Plants and Gardens (NCCPG) was formed in 1980 after an inaugural conference, which was held under the auspices of the Royal Horticultural Society.

One of the main aims of the NCCPG was to set up National Collections of plants from specific genera, particularly those which were considered to be endangered. There are now over 600 National Collections throughout Britain, in locations varying from botanic gardens to nurseries and small private gardens. Five of these National Collections are devoted to geraniums, the oldest established being at the University Botanic Garden at Cambridge and the most recent at Catforth Gardens, Lancashire.

UNIVERSITY BOTANIC GARDEN, CAMBRIDGE

by Dr Peter F. Yeo

The geranium collection at Cambridge developed gradually as a result of Peter Yeo's work on the taxonomy of particular groups, begun in the 1960s. By the time the NCCPG was formed, Yeo had become interested in growing geranium species from all parts of the world. The collection had reached a size which enabled it to be designated immediately as a National Collection. Since the aim was to clarify species definitions and species relationships, the collection was not confined to species of horticultural value, and most new acquisitions were first grown in the Research Section of the Garden, which is not open to the public.

In 1977 a group of display beds was planted up near the Rock Garden, partly based on a new classification of the genus by Yeo, and intended to show the range of variation in the genus. In addition, the existence of the research collection led to an enhancement of the displays of *Geranium* in other parts of the Garden (the Rock Garden, Woodland Area, Systematic Beds and the Herbaceous Island Beds).

Although geraniums are easy to grow, *Geranium incanum* and *G. traversii* do not usually survive Cambridge winters, and *G.* 'Russell Prichard' usually succumbs after a few years. *G. lambertii* 'Swansdown' is very difficult to keep in Cambridge. *G. yunnanense* has survived in pots but has disappeared from the Rock Garden, and is reported difficult in southern England by others. Members of Section Polyantha (*G. polyanthes*, *G. hispidissimum*, *G. strictipes*) which form massive rootstocks, are temperamental, being easy to establish but liable to die off without warning.

CAMBRIDGE PARKS DEPARTMENT, CHERRY HINTON HALL

by John Hobson

The inaugural meeting of the Cambridgeshire NCCPG, which I attended as an individual, was held in 1983. My job as the nursery manager of the Cambridge Parks Service (as it was then) gave me the opportunity to approach the City to request that we find room within the nursery to hold a National Collection.

I thought the most constructive plan would be to hold a cultivar collection of a genus already represented at the Cambridge Botanic Garden by a species collection. The first choice was *Geranium*, mainly because I had been growing garden-worthy types since 1955. The main advantage of this arrangement of course is that it allows for the study of the genus in a convenient geographical area.

The plot was first marked out in March 1984; at the same time members of the NCCPG began to scan catalogues for the first cultivars to go into the collection. I remember that of the first ten purchased, seven were wrongly named – I was glad of my thirty years experience. A piece of ground $65\frac{1}{2} \times 65\frac{1}{2}$ft ($20 \times 20$m) – about 478 sq yd (400sq m) – was thought to be enough to begin with. This was bordered on two sides by tall hedges, the open sides facing approximately north-east and north-west. The pH was found to be alkaline at 7.8 and the top soil had departed long ago for parts unknown! The soil has gradually been improved and the size of the plot has increased. The soil conditions are cold and sticky in winter, and slow to warm up.

It has been interesting over the years to take note of those varieties which have the longest-lasting foliage, and also those which show seasonal changes of foliage colour. The *Geranium macrorrhizum* cultivars all have reliable autumn and winter tints and are more or less evergreen – perhaps *G.m.* 'Ingwersen's Variety' has the edge over the others. G. × *magnificum* will usually produce autumn colour,

although it is not evergreen. The G. × *oxonianum* types are reliably evergreen, as is *G. endressii* 'Wargrave Pink', which will also produce the odd flower or two throughout the winter if the east wind stays away.

Interesting leaf forms are found in *Geranium renardii* 'Whiteknights' and *G. traversii elegans*. The former has mounds of grey-green foliage which are velvety to the touch, and the latter has attractive leaves of silver-grey. A more unusual type of geranium foliage is displayed by *G. incanum* var. *multifidum*, with very finely divided leaves in light green. *G. sylvaticum* 'Album' can be a very good foliage plant; it seems to be most attractive just before coming into bloom. Perhaps my favourite geraniums for spring growth are the *G. clarkei* cultivars, *G.c.* 'Kashmir White', 'Kashmir Purple' and 'Kashmir Pink'. However, I am also looking out anxiously for the first signs of *G. wallichianum* 'Buxton's Variety'.

PAGES 80–1
Part of the National Collection of geraniums at Cherry Hinton Hall, Cambridge, including *G. sanguineum* var. *striatum*, *G.* × *oxonianum* 'A.T. Johnson' and *G. clarkei* 'Kashmir White'

COOMBLAND GARDENS, WEST SUSSEX

by Rosemary Lee

82

My interest in hardy geraniums began in 1983 when we started planting and developing our large garden, which now extends to 5 acres (2ha). These wonderful plants had initially been suggested as a suitable underplanting for old roses. I learned very quickly that there was such a variety of form and type that there was a geranium for virtually every condition and situation within the garden. Naturally I fell in love with the family. Here was a group of plants that were not generally troubled by pests or diseases, nor were they fussy as to soil.

Our collection was designated and recognised as one of the National Collections in the spring of 1989. We now have one hundred and nineteen species and fifty-one cultivars. Several more cultivars are undergoing trials and I hope some of these will be worthy and sufficiently different to be named.

The soil in our garden varies but is mostly heavy to medium clay, and it is slightly acid. The collection is planted on a north-facing slope within the nursery. This is laid out in a 'field' situation, which enables the visitor to see the geraniums en masse in their glory when in flower. It is also easy to compare their form and individual merits. Hybridisation can and does happen, but this is exciting – one always hopes that a really good new variety might appear.

The alpine types do not do as well in the field situation, being more liable to disappear during a wet winter. Accordingly, these are kept safely in clay pots in a separate alpine area.

In addition to the main collection, we have planted areas of the garden with as many different geraniums as possible. Apart from keeping populations pure, it is also an excellent way of demonstrating their use in the border, wild garden, woodland, and as much-needed ground-cover plants.

The 'Kashmir Pink' form of G. *clarkei* has flowers of a clearer, truer pink than other geraniums

CATFORTH GARDENS, PRESTON, LANCASHIRE
by Judith Bradshaw

Ours is the most northerly of the National Collections, situated on the Fylde plain, north of Preston in Lancashire, in a one-acre garden. Having always gardened on heavy clay, we could hardly believe the rich, heavy loam we found when we moved here. We can garden throughout the winter without compacting the soil. About 12in (30cm) below this loam, a heavy clay subsoil retains water during the summer. We mulch every spring to retain a good crumbly soil – the mulch also helps during drought and cuts down weeding. Our main problems are the savage salt-laden gales which repeatedly batter the garden each winter; and our flat land, combined with heavy winter rainfall, giving the damp conditions disliked by so many plants. We combat the winter dampness by digging in grit, mulching with pea gravel and more grit, and constructing raised beds for plants that need extra good drainage. Most of our planting is done in spring, otherwise even completely hardy plants fail to establish.

Geraniums grow well here, it being more lush than in drier parts of the country. When I see plants in the drier east and even in the southwest, where summers are often drier, the plant and leaf size are so much smaller that I can hardly recognise them as the same ones I grow. Even though spring growth is about a month later than in the south, plants here retain their freshness and vigour into the autumn.

Until moving here we had only a few geraniums, most given to us by my father, but after reading Graham Stuart Thomas' *Plants for Ground Cover* (1970) I realised there were many more – though for some time I was unaware just how many more. We were looking for ground cover to fill in spaces between new plantings, so we began collecting some of the varieties he recommended. I was so attracted by these that I searched for others, until I became so enamoured that I was collecting every type I

could find. When I had about 150 (a mixture of species, subspecies and cultivars), I applied for National Collection status. Permission for this was given in 1991.

I have found that geraniums are very trouble-free plants. The only ones I have to take particular care of are the South African and Canary Island species, plus *Geranium traversii*. None of the South African species are reliably hardy here in the winter. Having tried them in various sheltered parts of the garden, they sometimes come through a mild winter but succumb the next year. Now, they are either grown in pots and moved into a cold greenhouse in autumn, or dug up and overwintered in the greenhouse. They have survived temperatures of 21°F (−6°C) inside, so it must be the cold winds and dampness they dislike.

Geranium maderense dies at the first sign of frost so it is kept in a heated frame over winter, and unless we have a hot summer it often refuses to flower outside. *G. canariense* is easier. In a large pot it flowers well outdoors and so far has survived in a cold greenhouse over winter. *G. palmatum* shows a complete disregard for our winters. I've grown plants outside now for five years, completely unprotected, in temperatures down to 14°F (−10°C). They not only survive but show increased vigour after a long period of frost, and then flower for weeks in summer, in either sun or semi-shade. Their evergreen rosettes also look very attractive in winter.

All the varieties of *Geranium endressii*, *G. versicolor* and *G. × oxonianum* are completely evergreen here. The spent flowers and old leaves are usually tidied away in autumn, and they then make spreading clumps of fresh leaves all winter. They are very good in shade and although there may not be so many flowers, they last longer and the colours blend well with woodland plants. They have a good mulch every spring. Another group of shade-loving

The petals of G. x *oxonianum* 'Thurstonianum' are compressed to give rich colour over many months from midsummer. The early flowers often produce petaloid stamens to give a semi-double appearance

geraniums includes G. *phaeum*, G. *reflexum* and G. × *monacense*, with flowers that follow the spring bulbs, and look well with arums, emerging ferns and hostas. These are also evergreen.

In contrast, *Geranium macrorrhizum* is not even semi-evergreen here in most winters. Even if a few leaves are retained, they look rather scruffy. However, it is still rated as an excellent ground-cover plant, the new leaves emerging in late winter, and its rhizomes keep down the weeds. It does good service even in the inhospitable places that other plants reject.

An evergreen geranium we are very fond of is *Geranium pyrenaicum*, also the white form and the cultivar G.*p.* 'Bill Wallis'. Their rounded grey-green leaves form charming rosettes, and they flower throughout the summer, often scrambling through nearby shrubs.

Although few geraniums insist on choice positions, new plants are given the best conditions for growing on until they can be propagated — they can then be tried experimentally in various places. The most temperamental plants are the forms of G. × *riversleaianum*, which only thrive in a well-drained sunny border, where they then stay green all winter.

Many geraniums grow well on the edge of woodland or in the shade from buildings, provided the soil is not too dry. G. *albanum*, G.

erianthum, G. *eriostemon* (now G. *platyanthum*), G. *nervosum*, G. *swatense* and G. *wallichianum* all enjoy these conditions, associating well with dicentras, hostas, rhododendrons and later, hydrangeas and hebes, through which they weave and scramble.

The only geraniums that have ever suffered mildew here are the various forms of G. *pratense*. They often look quite scruffy after flowering, so they get cut back hard, which produces fresh leaves for the rest of summer. G. × *magnificum* is also cut back after flowering, so that its flopping leaves do not swamp other plants. Given this treatment it looks attractive until autumn, when its leaves often colour well. Autumn colour here is not as predictable as in other parts of the country which experience greater extremes of temperature, but one geranium that never fails to give a lovely display is G. *wlassovianum*. Its large leaves turn rich shades of red and purple. The annual geraniums, G. *ocellatum* and G. *lucidum* also colour well. Although G. *ocellatum* does grow and flower outside, the flowers are more profuse and much larger when grown in the greenhouse.

National Collection holders are asked to grow at least three plants of each type, and to distribute plants to prevent losses. Luckily we have a garden large enough to accommodate three of each plant, and having the nursery enables me to have many more plants in reserve, as we try to offer at least 100 varieties for sale each year. As soon as I propagate a few plants of a new geranium I distribute some to other collectors. In this way rare plants are less likely to be lost to cultivation, and there is another source of supply if I lose my original plants.

We are currently constructing a special display bed for the collection, but we shall still continue to grow them in the garden in association with other plants, because this is how we prefer to see and enjoy them. There are now over 260 different geraniums in the collection, but having just obtained a copy of the *Geranium Family Species Check List*, there is obviously plenty of scope for years of happy geranium hunting ahead.

EAST LAMBROOK MANOR GARDEN

South Petherton, Somerset

As the late Margery Fish did so much to popularise the use of geraniums through her books, articles and talks, it is very appropriate that one of the National Collections should be located in the garden she created at East Lambrook Manor, now revitalised by Andrew and Dodo Norton.

It is a very large collection, comprising over 160 species, plus primary hybrids and garden cultivars, which bring the number to well over 250 – and increasing all the time. Andrew Norton makes a point of adding every possible new variety, not because they are all distinctive and garden-worthy (indeed many are not), but for the sake of completeness, as it is essentially a reference collection.

Many of the species are arranged in special display beds near the entrance, others are integrated into the main garden, as living examples of good siting and association.

Upwards of eighty varieties are offered in the mail order catalogue, and small stocks of others are sometimes available to personal callers at the nursery. Items in the catalogue are cross-indexed to references about them in Margery Fish's books.

8

GERANIUMS IN NORTH AMERICA

Some very attractive native forms of geraniums have crossed the Atlantic from North America to seek their fortunes over in the British Isles. Two that are particularly valued in my garden are *Geranium maculatum* and *G. oreganum*. The former has real star quality – the dark stems set off the elegantly shaped leaves and the soft mauve-pink flowers and give it a special grace. A native of New England, where it grows in damp woods and meadows, it is obviously happiest in

A North American native, *G. oreganum* commands attention with its large striking flowers of bright pink

similar conditions, but is obliging enough to grow in mixed borders as well. The pure white form is even more worthy of a favourable site. *G. oreganum* is a plant with a strong presence, whose very large, flat flowers in bright pink are an immediate attraction.

A number of native American geraniums are usefully gathered together in a special area of the University Botanic Garden in Vancouver, which includes such garden-worthy plants as *Geranium richardsonii* and *G. erianthum*. However, there is also an increasing American interest in collecting and growing geraniums from other parts of the world – an interest which became more strongly focussed by the formation of a Pacific Northwest Group of the Hardy Plant Society.

The two members largely responsible for setting this up, for organising annual study weekends, and contributing to the main Society's seed exchange, were Marvin Black and Dennis Thompson. Sadly, they have died in recent years, but another founder member, Dan Douglas, still runs a nursery with his wife, Evie, at Snohomish, Washington. Further interest is now being generated by the Hardy Plant Society of Oregon and the Perennial Alliance in Seattle, both affiliated to the HPS. Several other members, some of whom also belong to the Geraniaceae Group of the British Pelargonium and Geranium Society, have contributed information about their experiences in growing hardy geraniums under many different conditions.

Elaine Baxter Cantwell is the former editor of the Geraniaceae Group News (UK) and lives and gardens in West Islip, New York. Her garden is in USDA Zone 7–6, in which the lowest winter temperatures are –17.8°C (0°F) for short periods, with no snow cover, going up to a maximum summer temperature of 90°F (32°C). Because of the waterfront location, there is also high humidity, and wind.

Elaine thinks that geraniums should be touted as, 'the ideal every-place perennial'. She grows some thirty varieties and has found them amazingly adaptable, and suitable for mixed planting in all areas of the garden.

After initially introducing geraniums as ground cover under deciduous azaleas, she has tried out newly acquired varieties in all sorts of situations, and was delighted to find that G. *clarkei* 'Kashmir White' does almost equally well on a dry slope as in a moist area in part shade. Her favourite geranium is G. *pratense* 'Striatum', which she deadheads to prolong the flowering season.

At Rainforest Gardens in British Columbia, Elke and Ken Knechtel run a nursery which stocks around 100 varieties of geranium – they

Large colonies of G. *maculatum* are found growing in damp situations in North America, but this coolly elegant plant is quite adaptable to being grown under garden conditions, if not too dry

have had to move to bigger premises! Some winters are mild there, others can be −4°F (−20°C) with snow cover. Winter wet does not suit some of the more delicate forms, but *Geranium sessiliflorum* comes through safely. *G. maculatum* is a great success, the *G. clarkei* forms are spectacular and long flowering, and *G. phaeum* remains evergreen. Others which do well are *G. psilostemon*, especially the 'Bressing-ham Flair' variety, and the several forms of *G. sanguineum*.

An all-time favourite is *Geranium wlas-sovianum*, highly rated for autumn colour,

Geranium wlassovianum has a long season of foliage interest, with the bright chocolate centre of the young leaves spreading and becoming paler as they mature, eventually going bright red in autumn to accompany late-season flowers

which is supplied to a lesser degree by *G. macrorrhizum* and *G. × cantabrigiense* if they are grown in sun. The Knechtels have recently introduced two new forms of *G. × oxonianum* – *G. × o.* 'Anmore' and *G. × o.* 'Phoebe Noble', named after the plantswoman in whose garden on Vancouver Island they were found.

Dan and Evie Douglas run Cricklewood Nursery in Snohomish, Washington. The summer temperatures are mostly 65–75°F (18–24°C) with many overcast days but not much actual rain. The winters are usually 25–45°F (−4–7°C) with a lot of rain, drizzle and fog. The springs are cool and wet, but the autumns are warm, sunny and dry. The soil is very sandy and acid.

Geranium macrorrhizum is grown for ground cover, it is evergreen in mild winters and colours well in autumn. *G. palmatum* seeds around and

withstands below-zero temperatures in winter. *G. procurrens*, although a wanderer, is valued for its late autumn colour with the Michaelmas daisies. *G. renardii* is partially evergreen.

Cricklewood was one of the nurseries I visited a few years ago when I was giving talks in America, and I was entranced by the informal way in which geraniums were growing in the garden. There were many different colour forms of *Geranium pratense*, including slightly variant examples of *G. p.* 'Mrs Kendall Clark'. The late Dennis Thompson also had a plot of ground there for growing on geraniums, and named a particularly striking form of *G. sanguineum* as *G. s.* 'Cricklewood', after the nursery.

John Whittlesey runs Canyon Creek Nursery in Oroville CA which has a flourishing mail order business across the country. Situated in the lower foothills of the Sierra Nevada, the nursery is subjected to very hot summers, which can be over 105°F (41°C) for ten days in a row; and there is also the occasional wildfire to contend with! The winters are relatively mild, ideal for the less hardy perennials.

John finds that the low-growing forms of geraniums do particularly well for him, mounding up attractively. As safe recommendations for any climate he suggests the various forms of *Geranium* × *cantabrigiense*, and *G. endressii*, plus *G.* × *riversleaianum*, especially *G.* × *r.* 'Mavis Simpson'. *G. sanguineum* stands up well to full sun, and favourite forms are the very large-flowered *G. s.* 'Cedric Morris' and *G.s.* var. *striatum*.

Robin Parer is a garden writer and plantswoman who travels the world to find rewarding forms of geranium. Her nursery at Kentfield, California specialises in these, and also erodiums – but they are only available to personal callers, not by mail order.

The nursery is in USDA Zone 9, with average minimum temperatures of 20–30°F (−7 to −1°C), so almost all geraniums are hardy there. The very extensive catalogue includes the hardiness of plants in various zones. Care is needed in hot climates to position them so that they get some afternoon shade. Because of the favour-

able climate, propagation is not so restricted to specific seasons, although it has been found that *Geranium cinereum* and its forms respond best to spring propagation. However, it also means that climatic conditions are not variable enough to produce much in the way of autumn colour, except for *G. wlassovianum*.

Carol Roller lives at Vista in southern California about sixty miles north of the Mexican border, and ten miles inland from the Pacific. Although there are breezes from the ocean, the area is also subject to a particularly unpleasant form of wind called Santa Ana which roars in from the east and can make it breathlessly hot in summer. Sometimes there is frost in winter. It is a very dry area, normal rainfall is only 9–10in (23–25cm) a year, with very low humidity.

In spite of these adverse conditions – which includes plants being undermined by gophers! – Carol enjoys experimenting with new varieties of geranium and finding ways of adapting to their special requirements. *G. macrorrhizum* does well, but is less lush than in more favoured situations. *G. sanguineum* is fairly successful, *G. dalmaticum* grows but does not thrive, and the outstanding success is *G.* × *cantabrigiense* which blooms for most of the year. The North American varieties *G. richardsonii* and *G. maculatum* are grown with special attention to shading and watering.

There is a considerable amount of knowledge, experience and interest in growing geraniums in America, under widely differing conditions which include extremes of temperature, and great enterprise is shown in trying out new varieties. Over the years, a lot of this knowledge and experience has been shared with us both in correspondence and by visits. We have been greatly helped in compiling this section by a stream of letters, nursery catalogues and copies of articles from fellow enthusiasts. In particular, we would like to thank Robin Parer whose unique nursery specialises in *Geraniaceae*.

PAGES 90–1
G. x *riversleaianum* 'Mavis Simpson' softens an area of brick paving with a generous mat of silvery grey leaves studded with white-flecked, pink flowers

9

GERANIUMS IN AUSTRALIA

by Trevor Nottle

'Geraniums' got rather a lot of attention in the early gardening literature of Australia; unfortunately, for the purposes of this book, it was all about the wrong sort of 'geraniums'. Settlers arriving from England and Europe by sailing ship via the Cape of Good Hope brought many cuttings and even pot-plants as cabin luggage, but the 'geraniums' among them were all species or hybrid pelargoniums.

The geranium species native to Australia are all indifferent and weedy; most commonly their only commendable attribute is that they make useful fodder plants in mixed pastures. *Geranium molle*, an annual, and *G. pilosum* (syn. *G. dissectum* var. *australe*), a perennial, are both widespread. They are low, scrambling plants which form loose mats of hairy, round, indented green leaves and carry insignificant pink or white blooms. There is nothing about them that would have attracted the attention of the few free settlers who could have afforded the luxury of making a flower garden, when all around them were people desperately trying to grow enough edible crops to feed their families between the arrival of infrequent supply ships.

Even once the hardest years had gone by, and a middle class had developed with some leisure time and the means to make gardens, hardy cranesbills seem to have been ignored or at least unrecorded until *Geranium superba* appeared in the 1857 list of John Rule's Victoria Nursery at Richmond in Melbourne. It is unclear what Rule's *G. superba* was, as he simply lists it in his thirty-two-page catalogue of trees and shrubs for sale. It is tantalising to speculate whether or not it was one of the larger flowered members of the pratense group. However, his 1860 list is notable for its offering of *Geranium robertianum*, which marked the beginning of a long and inglorious history of infiltration and invasion by this plant.

Somewhat later, in 1864, *Geranium tuberosum* appeared in the lists of Handasyde, McMillan and Co, a seed warehouse in the city of Melbourne that also operated a nursery at Gardiner's Creek Road, Toorak. It was the age of exotic Asian and American trees and shrubs, so it is hardly surprising that such humble perennials as cranesbills were not imported by the few nurserymen who supplied the wants of fashion-conscious customers in the Australian colonies.

A latter-day Antipodean disciple of the Surrey School of garden style, Edna Walling was, and remains, an influential writer and garden maker from the 1930s until the 1950s. As a designer she was in great demand, particularly in Victoria where the mild climate enabled many English garden flowers to be cultivated successfully. As a journalist with a national magazine, *Australian Home Beautiful*, her ideas, favourite plants and plans reached a far wider population.

In *Gardens in Australia* (1943), she writes with enthusiasm of '*Geranium sanguineum album* with its glistening white flowers'. To make a 'glorious group' she recommends adding *G. grandiflorum*. Miss Walling had rather a thing at this stage of her career about old-fashioned flowers, so it is tempting to wonder if she had found in her 'clear, almost blue' G. *grandiflorum* a transplanted descendant of John Rule's *Geranium superba*. She was certainly known for collecting plants she liked from old derelict gardens and from the gardens of her Establishment clients; these she propagated, wrote about, and sold from her nursery. In *A Gardener's Log* (1948) she again mentions 'that dear little rock geranium *Geranium sanguineum album*'; but by this time plant quarantine laws had been enacted, and the developing vogue for English-style gardens and perennial borders was nipped in the bud by the costs and difficulties of importing plants.

The impact of these events was that none of the other geraniums found in the influential post-war English gardening magazines and books could be obtained in Australia. Even major new directions in gardening made little headway against the conservatism imposed by the costs to nurserymen of plant quarantine. For instance, the rage for old-fashioned roses that started between the wars and spread like wildfire after 1945, took nearly twenty years to show up in Australian rose catalogues. What chance then for comparatively marginal money-spinners such as geraniums?

A few determined alpine gardeners and RHS members raised seed imported from England, Scotland and New Zealand, and while the resultant plants were certainly swapped and traded among keen gardeners, the quantities made available by this means were negligible in commercial terms. Nonetheless, around this time, species listed as *Geranium pratense*, G. *ibericum*, G. *himalayense* and G. *grandiflorum* began to circulate, particularly from the well-known Norgate's Flower Farm at Trentham in central Victoria. It seems that stocks varied from year to year, or was it that the names were changed according to the tides of botanical opinion? Denis Norgate also offered then, as he still does, G. × *riversleaianum* 'Russell Prichard', G. *sanguineum*, G. *incanum* and G. *endressii* 'Wargrave Pink'.

Around this time, alpine nurseries began to appear, and to send out plants by mail order.

Several at least were run by European refugees with experience and contacts that enabled them to obtain seeds of more unusual varieties. Charlie Szabo of Stirling in South Australia raised stocks of the diminutive bronze-leaved *Geranium sessiliflorum* 'Nigricans', G. *renardii* and also the elegant silver G. *traversii* var. *elegans*. These varieties gradually spread among keen growers and specialist nurserymen. The attraction of growing others, such as the splendid G. *anemonifolium* and the hugely magnificent G. *maderense* may well have been the challenge set down by the difficulties reported in growing them in England! The fillip of having 'A letter from Australia' published in *The Garden* or one of the other learned society journals was sufficient spur to many gardeners to try such grand curiosities.

Slowly the stock of geraniums available to Australian gardeners grew. Ken Gillanders who operates Woodbank Nursery at Longley in Tasmania began to raise seed and import named clones. His current stock stands at seventeen varieties, after twenty years and more of collecting and growing. Ken rates *Geranium cinereum* 'Lawrence Flatman' as his most favoured variety, and reports that under his cool climate conditions, G. *phaeum* var. *lividum* and G. *tuberosum* are the most difficult to grow. Among his selections, G. × *lindavicum* 'Apple Blossom', G. *cinereum* 'Ballerina', G. × *cantabrigiense* and G. × *c*. 'Biokovo' show that he is keeping pace with new developments and trying them out locally.

Starting a few years after Ken, I grew many geraniums from seed obtained through the Hardy Plant Society and its Geranium Study Group. Joy Jones (then Joy Forty) kindly encouraged me with letters and packets of seed. I cannot claim to have been highly successful. *Geranium thunbergii* prospered all too well; G. *nodosum* seeds about pleasingly as do G. *versicolor* and G. *macrorrhizum* – the latter in

PAGE 94–5
The sumptuous double flowers of G. *himalayense* 'Plenum' (also known as G.*h*. 'Birch Double') are sterile, which ensures a longer flowering season

several colour variants. But stocks of several double forms, imported with the aid of Dick Kitchingman, failed to thrive in our hot, dry summers even with attentive watering. I think the extreme dryness of the air, combined with the heat, simply fatigued the plants to the point of collapse without recovery. This did not stop me from trying again with these, and I re-imported *G. pratense* 'Plenum Album', *G.p.* 'Plenum Caeruleum', *G.p.* 'Plenum Violaceum' and *G. himalayense* 'Plenum', along with *G. clarkei* 'Kashmir White' and *G. pratense* 'Mrs Kendall Clark' from a commercial source. The plants that survived quarantine were quickly passed on to several growers who live in more favourable climates, and I retained plants for myself to experiment with. 'Mrs Kendall Clark' has grown very well in sandy soil heavy with water, but *G. clarkei* 'Kashmir White' and *G. himalayense* 'Plenum' have barely survived in similar conditions with slightly better drainage, higher up a slope. Seed-raised *G. cataractarum*, with almost white flowers, has become a persistent weed in my nursery patch.

Other amateurs contacted me after the publication of my book *Growing Perennials* in 1984. Moraig Godfrey who lived at Queanbeyan on the outskirts of Canberra, befriended Pat Hart and May Brett over their mutual interest in hardy perennials including geraniums, while over on the other side of the continent, Betty Swainson tried to grow whatever she could obtain for her garden near Albany, West Australia. Esmond Jones, then living at Balmain on the shores of Sydney Harbour, tried many seed packets too, and found like the rest of us that there are some very weedy geraniums getting about in overseas seed lists.

Despite our very varied range of soils and climatic conditions, we found that the varieties so popular in the cool, temperate gardens of Europe, England and North America were moderately difficult to grow. Each had successes with members of the Pratense clan, the Palmatum group, the Macrorrhizum group and the various forms of *Geranium sanguineum*. After these, there were individual successes with *G.*

traversii, *G. psilostemon*, *G. renardii* and the colour forms of *G. phaeum*. As the plants were seed-raised there was some variation from the parent material, enough to make us wish that we could afford to import more plants of named clones.

Rene Coffield of Creswick in central Victoria was operating from this time. Rene runs a small nursery which specialises in alpine plants and small bulbs. She has offered from time to time, plants of the smaller-growing geraniums, including the various colour forms of *G. sanguineum* as well as *G. traversii* and *G. sessiliflorum* 'Nigricans'. Often her seed sources were overseas rock garden clubs, and while her correspondents were able to supply her with seed from the best named varieties, she was always conscientious about not claiming that her plants were the named varieties themselves. Nonetheless, to collectors starved of the 'real' plants available in England and elsewhere, she did offer opportunities for enthusiasts to obtain some fine plants, and her efforts were much appreciated by her discerning clientele.

Just at the point where interest in geraniums could have waned, a series of events occurred that led to an upturn of interest. At the end of the 1960s, five new nurseries began to import plants and seed for their mail order businesses, and the towns in the highlands of New South Wales and Victoria around the Australian Alps began to boom, creating new markets for temperate zone plants.

Michael Pitkin runs a nursery at Viburnum Gardens, 25 miles (40km) north-west of Sydney, with what sounds like the ideal address for a nursery – Arcadia! He offers a wide range of geraniums and is continuing to try new species as seed becomes available. Michael has raised plants grown from field-collected seed. Three plants in particular have attracted attention, though their names are not yet clearly established: one is a vigorous plant to 40in (100cm) with rose-lilac flowers – field notes indicate its affinity with *Geranium chinense*; another is known as 'China Blue' and came from seed collected from Crow Creek in Alaska; while the third is tentatively labelled as *G. siberica* until it can be definitely identified. It is described by Michael as having 'fine, soft blue flowers'. Plants of all three have been sent to England so their status can be further investigated. The best of the hybrids raised by Michael is a fine slate-blue which has *G. phaeum* in its breeding. Summer in Sydney is hot and often oppressively humid; under these conditions Michael finds that *G. psilostemon*, *G.* × *magnificum*, *G. cinereum*, *G.c.* 'Ballerina', *G. endressii* and forms such as *G.e.* 'Wargrave Pink', and *G.* × *riversleaianum* 'Russell Prichard', all die out after a few seasons.

Michael has produced a very interesting summary of his experiences in growing geraniums in this particular area, with detailed recommendations for individual cultivation in a wide range of circumstances.

At his nursery there is very little rainfall; winter day-time temperature is 52°F (11°C), going up to 104°F (40°C) in summer. The main problem is the high humidity in summer. However, by trial and error he is gradually building up an extensive range of geraniums which will flourish in these conditions. So far they include:

Geranium asphodeloides	G. phaeum
G. cataractarum	G. pratense
G. himalayense	G. rubescens
G. ibericum	G. sanguineum
G. macrorrhizum	G. sylvaticum
G. maderense	G. versicolor
G. × oxonianum	G. viscosissimum

Many of these are grown in several forms, and named varieties.

Southward in the cool, damp hills that ring Melbourne, David Glenn established his Lambley Nursery at Olinda, and Graham Cooke set up his Romantic Cottage Garden nursery near Frankston. At nearby Dromana overlooking Port Phillip Bay, Clive Blazey's Digger's Plants completes a trio of entrepreneurial nurseries.

All grow a range of geraniums with offerings varied from year to year according to the availability of seed, and luck with propagation.

David has family connections in the trade in England, and a son who has been plant hunting in China, so his offerings tend to be wide-ranging. The others seek out sources of plants illustrated in popular overseas gardening magazines and books, and those they feel will stand local conditions well. Trips to Chelsea, other major flower shows and famous gardens further inform their choice of plants to introduce. Special mention must be made of *Geranium* × 'Criss Canning', a hybrid of *G. pratense* × *G. himalayense*, raised by David Glenn and named after his partner. It grows vigorously, making a mound of foliage, and masses of large, deep blue flowers throughout spring and summer.

Further west and into a drier, hotter climatic zone akin to the Mediterranean, Felicity Kent has lately set up her Rokewood Nursery at Mount Barker in South Australia. She makes a point of growing all her plants from seed, and scans seed lists and floras to match likely plants from around the world with the local climate. Although not strong on geraniums, her catalogue does include varieties which have been well tested in her own garden. What is exciting about Felicity is not so much her list, though very useful to local gardeners, but her attitude; she persists in her search for perennials that suit conditions in her area and will no doubt unearth some unusual things yet – hopefully geraniums among them.

It would be remiss to end, leaving the impression that amateurs have left the field, and that everything to do with geraniums in Australia is being done by commercial growers. There are at least two amateurs living in the foothills of the Australian Alps who are hard at work raising all manner of seed and sharing the resulting seedlings around among other enthusiasts.

Craig Irving has his large (and growing) garden amid a cool-climate vineyard near Euroa and seems to grow just about everything that appears on Jim and Jenny Archibald's lists, including geraniums. A young man, he has made a strong start and as his worldwide network grows, he is obtaining seed from a wide variety of sources.

Robyn Rohrlach gardens in the town of Yac-kendandah in north-eastern Victoria, not far from Euroa. Robyn has a strong network of gardening pen-friends, especially on the West Coast of the USA and in New Zealand. In both countries she is well-known among enthusiasts for species irises, but her interest also covers wild forms of many other flowers, including geraniums and erodiums. Her friends, knowing this, frequently send packets of 'other' seed when they go out to collect iris seeds.

This picture of geraniums in Australia is very sketchy; this is a large country and many keen gardeners work in isolation from other enthusiasts. The climate ranges from tropical to cool temperate and there are vast areas of desert; some areas get reasonable summer rains, others receive none or suffer torrential downpours from infrequent thunderstorms. The soils are largely old and degraded (geologically), contain almost no humus and hence dry out very rapidly. There are pockets of river loam and silt, and in the high rainfall areas some patches of rich 'mountain soil'; but even so, keen gardeners find it necessary to build their soils up with annual dressings of compost, mulch and manures.

Obviously there are many areas where geraniums will not grow at all, and others where even the toughest kinds are marginal, yet this has not deterred a growing band of enthusiasts from trying every geranium they can obtain. Given the necessity of letter writing on a grand scale and the frustrations and costs of importing plants (provided you can first locate a European nurseryman willing to export), the choice of geraniums at present available is a fair reflection of the intense interest in the genus in Australia which exists among a devoted band of collectors, garden designers and adventurous nurserymen.

The rich blues and mauves of G. × *magnificum* and colour forms G. *pratense* such as G.p. 'Striatum' make an elegant spectacle, complimented, amongst others, by G. × *oxonianum* 'Claridge Druce' and the starry flowers of G. *asphodeloides* (Plant material from Trevor Bath's garden)

10

GERANIUMS IN NEW ZEALAND

by Malcolm Shearer

Gardening patterns in New Zealand tend to be strongly influenced by those in Britain, probably because of the large number of evocative and seductively illustrated books that are produced there, and readily available here. The current fashion for the cottage garden style, and the increasing interest in the conservation of plants which were popular in the past, has revived interest in the true geranium.

Species like *Geranium pratense*, *G. himalayense* and *G. endressii* have been grown here for many years, probably brought by colonists in the latter half of the last century, together with a few hybrids such as *G. × magnificum* and *G. endressii* 'Wargrave Pink', but they were rarely available commercially. During the past five years, nurseries and garden centres have begun to stock a small but increasing range as interest and demand have risen. For the enthusiast, seed ordered from overseas sources has been the best way of obtaining new species. Obtaining varieties which do not come true from seed is a problem. The increased stringency of our plant-importation regulations, with strict and expensive quarantine and inspection procedures, has made the cost of importing plants too great for the amateur gardener. Fortunately a few commercial growers, responding to the increase in interest, have begun to import a wider range of varieties. In the last year, for example, I have been able to buy *G. × oxonianum* 'A.T. Johnson', *G. × cantabrigiense*, *G. × cantabrigiense* 'Biokovo' and *G. sanguineum* 'Album'.

The climate in Christchurch in the South Island of New Zealand is perhaps most similar to that of the south of England. Rainfall is about 26in (650mm) annually, mostly in winter and spring. Summers are warm and dry, with occasional hot föhn north-westerlies giving temperatures above 86°F (30°C). Winters are cool, with average temperatures of 52°F (11°C) and frequent frosts. Snowfalls in coastal areas are exceptional.

The nomenclature of geraniums is a problem. The large numbers of species, hybrids and varieties, and the subtle differences in leaf form and flower colour, make identification from description or even from colour photographs, uncertain. Where varieties have been recently imported, one can be fairly certain that the naming is correct. Where plants are obtained from older stock, with no clear provenance, confusion easily arises. Peter Yeo's book is my bible, and the photographs in Volume One of the Rix and Phillips *Perennials* have been helpful.

All the varieties I grow seem to be perfectly hardy under our conditions, except *Geranium incanum* and *G. traversii*. It is perhaps curious that *G. traversii* should be on the borderline of hardiness here, in Christchurch, since it is native to the Chatham Islands, a group about 400 miles due west. However, despite the bleak windswept conditions there, frosts are less severe.

For many dedicated gardeners like myself, the variation in foliage forms is one of the major charms of the genus. The difference in scale from the opulent fans of *Geranium palmatum* to the prim neatness of *G. cinereum*, or our own native

G. *sessiliflorum*, is fascinating. So, too, is the degree of leaf division – from the solid textured G. *renardii* to the laciness of G. *incanum* – these differences add greatly to the attraction, as does the colour variegation, whether it is the marbled bicolour of G. *orientalitibeticum* or the bronze-purple of G. *sessiliforum* 'Nigricans'. Under our conditions, autumn colouring is shown to a

limited extent by a few species like G. *psilostemon* and G. *macrorrhizum*, while G. *sessiliflorum* 'Nigricans' has the endearing habit of producing occasional leaves which turn bright orange as they age. Quite honestly though, none of the plants I grow show really spectacular changes of colour. At present I grow around sixty different species and hybrids.

11

A–Z LIST OF GERANIUMS IN CULTIVATION

Geraniums included in the following list are perennial except where otherwise stated. The specific name is followed by any synonym or other name under which it may masquerade; its place of origin (helpful when deciding suitable sites for planting); and its parentage, if of hybrid origin. Height and flower sizes may vary according to soil and situation and are only approximate. The flower size refers to the diameter.

A list of specialist nurseries is provided at the end of the book to assist in purchasing plants. In Britain, *The Plant Finder*, published by Headmain Ltd in association with the Hardy Plant Society, is an invaluable source of information. Seed lists of various specialist societies are also worth exploring – a pleasant pastime for dark winter evenings.

When recommending certain geraniums for the wild or woodland garden, it is appreciated that few of us are fortunate enough to possess such desirable areas, in which case read 'wild corner' or 'under a tree', but proceed with caution!

GERANIUM ALBANUM

Originates in the south-eastern Caucasus and adjacent parts of Iran. From a compact rootstock, *G. albanum* makes substantial mounds of almost evergreen leaves, divided to about halfway and somewhat irregular in outline, 12–18in (30–45cm) in height. Flowers 1in (2.5cm) carried on long thin trailing stems, rather shocking pink, veined magenta; lightly notched petals and attractive violet-blue anthers. An underrated plant, usually consigned to the wild garden but worthy of a place in the shrub border for its long flowering season, from early summer onwards. The colour is not easy to place, though is effective growing through violet-blue azaleas. Clumps can be divided, or raised from seed.

GERANIUM ALBIFLORUM

Originates from northern and central Asia and north-eastern Russia, and is a modest but charmingly dainty plant, sometimes confused with *G. sylvaticum* forma *albiflorum*. It grows to 12–18in (30–45cm) high and its chief attraction lies in the purplish-brown margins of the deeply-cut leaves, which resemble those of *G. sylvaticum*, and in the same purplish-brown colour of the stems and sepals. Small funnel-shaped flowers, white or pale lilac, veined with violet and with notched petals, are produced spasmodically over a long period. Although found growing in woods and on the sides of streams in the wild, it is not difficult to accommodate in the garden in light shade. Tucked in the front of a border, it associates well with white-flowered plants. It may be propagated by division or seed.

G. anemonifolium. See G. palmatum.

GERANIUM 'ANN FOLKARD'
(G. procurrens × G. psilostemon)

This is an outstanding sterile hybrid raised by Rev Oliver Folkard in Lincolnshire in 1973.

From a comparatively small crown, a mass of golden-yellow foliage emerges in spring, each leaf deeply cut into five or seven, with sharply-toothed lobes, turning greener with age. Very long, thin stems are continually produced all summer and have the advantage of being non-rooting, unlike its parent *G. procurrens*, which can be invasive. The sumptuous saucer-shaped flowers 1½in (4cm) are a rich dusky-purple suffused with pink and bluish tinges, like shot silk. Prominent black veins converge into a black central zone. It starts flowering in mid-summer and carries on until cut back by frost. 'Ann' luxuriates in a sunny position where her trailing stems can weave through suitable hosts. Compatible companions are provided by pink or yellow shrub roses, pink or lavender clematis, ballota, euphorbias and lavatera. 'Ann' needs room to spread but can make a stunning specimen subject, either in a large pot or isolated in paving. Plants can be carefully divided in spring,

G. 'Ann Folkard' is seen at its best grown in paving, where it can throw its arms about and display the rich jewel-like colours of the flowers, lightened by the golden over-tones of the new leaves

just when the foliage is showing, and these divisions soon become established.

G. 'Anne Thomson', see page 75 for a list of Alan Bremner's hybrids.

G. 'Apple Blossom'. See G. × *lindavicum*.

GERANIUM ARGENTEUM

Originally from the French Alps, Italy and Yugoslavia, this is a little gem for the well-drained rock garden, scree or trough in an open, sunny situation, or an alpine house. It needs a sparse, gritty diet, as in rich soil it will make more foliage at the expense of flowers. Neat 4–6in (10–15cm) rosettes of small, rounded,

Stylishly swept-back petals with Regency stripes give G. *aristatum* an individual look

deeply cleft silvery leaves are a perfect foil for the pale, flesh-pink, sometimes white, flowers 1in (2.5cm). The flowers often have a network of darker veins and slightly notched petals. These, standing well above the foliage and fluttering in the breeze, continue blooming all through summer. G. *argenteum* dislikes winter wet, and it is advisable to protect the crown with a pane of glass during that season. Rosettes can be carefully divided in spring; cuttings or root cuttings are another possibility. Seed is not freely set, and may not come true if G. *cinereum* or its forms are grown in proximity.

GERANIUM ARISTATUM

This originates from the mountains of Albania, southern Yugoslavia and north-western Greece. It is a distinguished hairy geranium of the G. *phaeum* group, forming hummocks of grey-green foliage 18–24in (45–60cm). The leaves are somewhat similar in shape to those of G. *phaeum* but lighter in colour and more coarsely toothed. Distinctive nodding flowers 1in (2.5cm) with strongly reflexed petals of palest lilac-pink, are enhanced by attractive Regency-striped veins from mid-summer to autumn. A reliable plant for sun or half shade which benefits from a severe cut-back when untidy, which produces new growth and further flowers. It can be propagated by division or seed. Natural dispersal is by a coil mechanism but I have never found any self-sown seedlings, and collected seed is reluctant to germinate although chipping the seed may help.

GERANIUM ASPHODELOIDES

A variable species developing substantial leafy mounds 18in (45cm) from a stout rootstock. The rounded, fresh green leaves are almost evergreen, and make good ground cover in sun

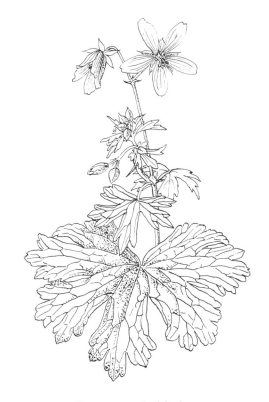

Geranium asphodeloides

or shade. It flowers all summer. G. *asphodeloides* is divided into three subspecies:

G. a. subsp. *asphodeloides* originating from southern Europe, has starry flowers about 1in (2.5cm) with gappy, narrow petals of white, pale pink or deep pink with darker veins.

G. a. subsp. *crenophilum* from the Lebanon and Syria is more evergreen. Flowers have more overlapping petals than the above, and are deep rosy-pink with darker veins.

G. a. subsp. *sintenisii* is a very free flowering plant from northern Turkey with pale pink or sometimes purple flowers. The whole plant is covered with red-tipped glandular hairs. A plant with pale pink flowers with crimped petals which I grew was identified by Dr Peter Yeo as this.

Two named varieties have recently been introduced by Axletree Nursery, and are described as follows by Dr David Hibberd:

G. a. 'Prince Regent' (1990) pale lilac petals, each with usually five more or less parallel dark lilac veins. 'Prince Regent' is an effective garden plant, and although individual flowers are only medium-sized, about 3/4in (2cm) in diameter, they are borne in profusion, and flowering starts early.

G. a. 'Starlight' (1990). The present clone was selected and given to us by Dr Yeo in 1987. It differs from 'Prince Regent' in having pure white flowers with broader petals and less deeply-divided leaves with a softer, bluish appearance, but resembles it in its freedom, earliness of flowering and long season.

All forms of G. *asphodeloides* benefit from being cut back in about mid-summer. They are easy to grow in sun but are not averse to half shade, spilling over low banks and walls. They also look well in the wild garden or in the front of a border, where their long flowering season is particularly valuable, especially when combined with their habit of weaving through other plants which may themselves have only a short season. They may be propagated by division or seed, but self-sown seedlings are usually abundant.

GERANIUM BICKNELLII

An annual, originally from North America and Canada. It is a fairly upright geranium, 6–18in (15–45cm) in height with thickish, dark green, rather shiny leaves, deeply cut into narrow, oblong segments, colouring yellow and red in the autumn. Small flowers 1/2in (1cm) occur in loose clusters, pale to rose-pink with dark-forked veins, notched petals and bluish anthers, with rather long-pointed fruits later. In its native habitat, G. *bicknellii* is fairly common in wooded areas and on roadsides, and might just qualify for a place in the wild or woodland garden.

GERANIUM BIUNCINATUM

Also an annual, this time from eastern Africa and the Arabian Peninsula, G. *biuncinatum* is a rather extraordinary cranesbill, with leaves divided into five or seven lobes, irregular in outline. The flowers are a striking deep pink, 3/4in (2cm), the petals overlapping with a black triangle at the base of each, forming a well defined centrepiece, edged finely with white. Sad to say I have never seen a single flower, as my plants are cleistogamous (ie without visible flowers, but forming seed through self-fertilisation); however, mine have reproduced each year from self-sown progeny. It has not so far been tried outside in the garden – perhaps this is the reason? All is not lost as the pale straw-coloured seed beaks are ridged and horned and thus of interest.

G. 'Black Ice', see page 75 for a list of Alan Bremner's hybrids.

GERANIUM BOHEMICUM

An annual from eastern and central Europe. It is a sprawling, hairy plant with pleasant, irregularly cut and wrinkled leaves. Its chief attraction is the colour of the flowers, which are about 3/4in (2cm), bright violet-blue with darker, forked veins and a pink central zone. It might prove a useful addition to the wild garden by virtue of this flower colour.

G. 'Brookside' (G. *pratense* x G. *clarkei*) has white-centred flowers of a good blue, shown here mingling informally with a white-flowered form of G. *asphodeloides*

GERANIUM 'BROOKSIDE'
(G. *pratense* × G. *clarkei* 'Kashmir Purple')

Another good introduction from Axletree Nursery (1989), originating on the research beds at Cambridge University Botanic Garden in 1970. A lovely, vigorous plant 12–18in (45–60cm), forming clumps of finely-cut leaves and large bowl-shaped flowers of a deep clear blue, paler at the centre. Mingling with G. *clarkei* 'Kashmir White' it makes a striking addition to the border. It is best to propagate by division, as very little seed is set, and this is unlikely to be true.

GERANIUM BRUTIUM

An annual originating from southern Italy, Sicily, the Balkan Peninsula and Turkey. It is a personal favourite, with light green, rounded leaves similar to those of G. *pyrenaicum* though less deeply divided, mounding up to 12in (30cm) or more. Flowers 1in (2.5cm) produced on some-what lax stems, are bright pink with prettily notched petals and blue-black anthers. This cheerful geranium has a place in odd corners of the border or large rock garden and looks par-ticularly at home in paving, where it self-sows moderately. It likes the sun but will live in shade, where the plants grow taller and the colour of the flowers is more intense. The seed is small and is possibly carried by the wind, as it has joined the 'garden escapes' in the field behind my gar-den. It has also appeared in the cracks of a neighbour's paving 100 yards (over 100m) up the lane, much to her delight and surprise!

GERANIUM CANARIENSE

Originally from the Canary Islands. It is a short-lived perennial bearing a striking rosette from a short stem, up to 6in (15cm). Numerous glossy green fragrant leaves up to 10in (25cm) or more across are produced on reddish-brown stems, resembling a large Herb Robert, about 24in (60cm) tall, but sometimes taller. Flowers about 1½in (4cm) have deep pink petals with three short, dark veins at the base and are rather widely spaced, whitish on the underside, with red anthers. It is free flowering from spring on-wards but is not very hardy, although may sur-vive in a dry sheltered corner on light soil. It is worth giving winter protection in the green-house or conservatory where it may live for three years or more, sometimes producing fresh rosettes. It can be propagated by seed. Seedlings need frequent repotting.

GERANIUM × CANTABRIGIENSE
(G. dalmaticum × G. macrorrhizum)

A sterile hybrid, raised at Cambridge University Botanic Garden in 1974, but which also occurs in the wild. Steadily forms dense mats of glossy, aromatic near-evergreen foliage and makes excel-lent ground cover. Leaves and flowers are midway between the parents. The abundantly produced flowers 1in (2.5cm) are bright pink and held above the foliage, which colours well in autumn.

G. × *c. 'Biokovo'*, which was found growing in the Biokovo Mountains of Yugoslavia, is less vigorous and makes looser mats, but the white, pink-tinged flowers are delightful. 'Biokovo' is less effective as ground cover.

Both are suited to the front of a border, large rock garden or beneath shrubs in sun or half shade. They are sterile, but easily propagated by detaching pieces of the runners.

GERANIUM CAROLINIANUM

An annual from North America, Canada and Mexico, this is an erect species 6–15in (15–38cm), growing from a rosette of rounded foliage. Later leaves are more deeply cut, with wedge-shaped segments. Funnel-shaped flowers ½in (1cm) or more, borne in compact clusters, are white or pale pink. Found in meadows and waste places in the wild, it probably has little garden value.

GERANIUM CATARACTARUM

Comes originally from southern Spain and Morocco. It is an endearing little plant with finely-cut, soft, aromatic evergreen leaves simi-lar to those of *G. robertianum* but lighter in col-our. Flowers ¾in (2cm) are funnel shaped, bright pink with orange-red anthers, from mid-summer to autumn. When grown in a trough in rather poor gritty soil it rarely exceeded 6in (15cm) but when tried in a dampish, half shaded corner of the garden, the result was a much taller plant 12in (30cm) with a lot more foliage but scarcely a flower. It has a fairly short life-span, though it can be reproduced from cuttings (which need winter protection) and seed.

G. 'Chantilly', see page 75 for a list of Alan Bremner's hybrids.

GERANIUM CINEREUM var. CINEREUM

From the central Pyrenees, this is an alpine species making tufts of small, cut, grey-green

108

leaves from rosettes 6in (15cm). Delicate cup-shaped flowers 1½in (4cm) appear in summer on rather frail trailing stems. They are pale pink with finely pencilled darker veins and notched petals, or in the case of *G.c.* var. *c.* 'Album', pure white. It needs well drained gritty soil in the rock garden, scree or trough. Covering with glass helps to protect the crowns from winter wet. Propagate by careful division, or from cuttings. Seed may be variable, especially if grown in proximity to *G. argenteum* or other forms of *G. cinereum*.

G.c. 'Ballerina' (*G. cinereum* var. *cinereum* × *G.c.* var. *subcaulescens*) A very attractive and popular rock garden plant raised by Bloom's Nurseries at Bressingham in Norfolk. Tufts of small ashy-green leaves similar to those of *G. cinereum* form quite wide mats, over which the flowers dance like true ballerinas. Produced all summer, the flowers are purplish-pink, 1¼in (3cm) across, and generously and darkly veined from a dark central zone. Propagation is best by division or cuttings, as few viable seeds are set.

Geranium cinereum 'Lawrence Flatman'

G.c. 'Lawrence Flatman' Another excellent introduction from Blooms Nurseries. It is similar to 'Ballerina' but the petals have a pronounced dark triangular mark towards the apex.

G.c. var. obtusilobum This was given to me many years ago by the late, sadly missed Ken Aslet when he was in charge of the alpine garden

section of the Royal Horticultural Society's garden at Wisley in Surrey. It was introduced by him from Mount Lebanon. The flowers stems emerge from a rosette of tiny, rounded, pale green leaves topped by delicate flowers 1in (2.5cm) across, which are near-white with just a hint of pink and produced all summer. The petals are oblong, notched with faint reddish veins. The plant is easily propagated by division or from seed, though it hybridises with others in this group.

G.c. var. subcaulescens Originally from the Balkan Peninsula, and central and north-eastern Turkey – and if you like a good splash of colour in the rock garden, this is a must. Darker in foliage than the forms of *G. cinereum* already described, it makes larger 9in (23cm) but tidy clumps of small, scalloped leaves covered from early summer onwards with brilliant crimson-magenta flowers. These are moderated by a black or near-black centre and dark veins, black stigmas and anthers. No problems in cultivation arise if it is grown in a sunny, well drained site in the rock garden, scree, front of the border, raised bed or paving. Other plants with silver of grey foliage, clear pink or pale blue flowers, help to cool this geranium's intense colour – but avoid scarlet at all costs! It is best propagated by division or cuttings as seed is not freely produced.

G.c. var. s. 'Giuseppii' is slightly less strident in colour than the type and lacks the distinct black centre, having only a darker area where the veins converge.

G.c. var. s. 'Splendens' has luminous, bright magenta-pink flowers with a blackish-red central zone and dark veins. It is a very eye-catching plant but not as robust as the previous two mentioned.

GERANIUM CLARKEI

Originally from Kashmir, there are three colour forms of this species available to gardeners. All have elegant leaves, deeply and narrowly cut with sharply pointed segments like snow flakes in outline. The plants are 12–18in (30–45cm) in height and flower from early to late summer.

G.c. 'Kashmir Pink' was introduced by Blackthorn Nursery, Kilmeston, Hampshire in 1990. It came from a seedling of *G. clarkei* 'Kashmir Purple' and has lovely soft pink flowers.

G.c. 'Kashmir Purple', sometimes sold mistakenly as *Geranium bergianum*, travels busily by underground rhizomes. It is rather too rampant for small gardens, though it is hard to resist the appeal of its large flowers 1½–2in (4–5cm). These are upward-facing, deep violet-purple, veined with lilac-pink and are lovely as massed ground cover for large areas, especially under pink or yellow shrub roses. Detached pieces of roots will provide a simple method of increasing stock, and seeds come true.

Geranium clarkei 'Kashmir White'

G.c. 'Kashmir White' (formerly known as *G. rectum album*) is less rampant than *G.c.* 'Kashmir Purple', spreading only moderately. Ethereal white, saucer-shaped flowers 1–1½in (2.5–4cm) are beautifully veined with greyish-lilac-pink giving a translucent appearance. Mingling with *G. himalayense* and *G.* 'Brookside', and backed by the taller *G. pratense* 'Striatum', it would provide a colourful group

for many weeks, with the addition of silver foliage plants to complete the picture.

G. 'Kashmir Blue'. See under 'K'.

GERANIUM COLLINUM

Originates from south-eastern Europe, central and eastern Turkey and western and central Asia. It is a loosely bushy plant up to 24in (60cm) in height, with finely cut grey-green, sharply toothed leaves. When emerging in spring, the foliage is often tinged with primrose yellow and pink. The saucer-shaped flowers are usually mid-pink but can be darker or lighter, sometimes red veined. It is a variable species, not particularly garden-worthy, but useful in the informal border or wild garden for its long flowering season and resistance to drought conditions. It can be propagated by division or seed.

GERANIUM DAHURICUM

From Asia, Russia and western China, this is a sprawling plant with small leaves finely cut into long, widely-spaced segments, sometimes red-edged, about 18in (45cm) in height. Saucer-shaped flowers 1in (2.5cm) are pale pink with fine red veins. Though not a spectacular species it has a long flowering period and is therefore welcome as an in-filler in the less tidy border or wild garden. It can be propagated by division or seed.

GERANIUM DALMATICUM

Originally from south-western Yugoslavia and Albania, this delightful dwarf cranesbill 4–6in (10–15cm) in height forms neat cushions of small, dark, glossy leaves which are aromatic, and deeply cut into five or seven wedge-shaped divisions, assuming brilliant autumn tints. In mid-summer it is covered with clear, shell-pink flowers 1in (2.5cm). It is suitable for the smallest rock garden, trough or paving in any reasonable soil, and will grow in sun or partial shade. Old plants seem to become tired of blooming, and

109

this is the time to split them up, replanting the younger pieces from the outside of the clump in fresh soil with the addition of a little bonemeal. It does not appear to set much seed.

G.d. 'Album' is not so vigorous as the type. The petals of this very desirable white form are just slightly tinged with pink.

G. 'Dilys'. See page 76 for a list of Alan Bremner's hybrids.

GERANIUM DONIANUM

From the Himalayas and China. Grows from a thick rootstock up to 16in (40cm) but often less, with quite large, marbled and deeply divided, silky leaves, kidney-shaped in outline. Its flowers are upward-turned, funnel-shaped and deep reddish-purple in colour. In my experience it is not long-lived, but would make an attractive addition to the rock garden if one could discover the formula for longevity. New plants are easily raised from seed, though all too often what you get from commercial sources under this name turns out to be *G. polyanthes*.

GERANIUM ENDRESSII

Originated from southern Europe and western Asia. Cultivated in gardens since 1812. It is one of the most frequently planted of all geranium species, and an excellent standby. It forms leafy clumps 18in (45cm) high with long, slender, creeping rhizomes. Individual leaves are fairly deeply cut into elegantly pointed divisions, light green in colour and almost evergreen. Copious, bright pink, funnel-shaped flowers $1\frac{1}{4}$–$1\frac{3}{8}$in (3–3.5cm) with notched petals, extend all summer and into autumn. However, by mid-summer, plants begin to look unkempt and benefit from being shorn to the ground. Provided they are kept moist, a fresh crop of foliage and flowers will carry on with renewed vigour. *G. endressii* makes splendid ground cover, not only for its attractive foliage, but because there is, as A.T. Johnson put it, '. . . scarcely a week when there will not be a pink bloom showing

Geranium endressii

somewhere'. Happy in sun or partial shade and almost any soil, it is a useful border plant. The only drawback is the promiscuous way in which it hybridises with *G. versicolor* and several other species. The resulting children are numerous and varied. The hybrids between *G. endressii* and *G. versicolor* have been named *G. × oxonianum* by Dr Yeo.

G.e. 'Wargrave Pink' (syn. 'Wargrave Variety') is a taller variety, up to 24in (60cm) and a strong grower. The warm salmon-pink flowers may be more acceptable to those who find the colour of *G. endressii* rather harsh.

GERANIUM ERIANTHUM

From eastern Siberia, Japan, Alaska and Canada (British Columbia), this is a variable plant 18–24in (45–60cm) in height with handsome leaves deeply divided into seven or nine overlapping lobes, each sharply and irregularly toothed, and colouring well in autumn. Delightful, large flowers 1–$1\frac{1}{2}$in (2.5–4cm) vary in colour from pale mauve-blue with strong, dark veining to deep purple with even darker veins. It is one of those quietly charming plants that looks at home in most places, in sun or half shade, associating pleasantly with blue-leaved hostas.

Flowering begins in early summer for several weeks and there are usually a few later blooms. Axletree Nursery has given one form the cultivar name of 'Neptune', which is a vigorous plant with lovely deep blue flowers. Propagation is by division or seed.

G. eriostemon. See G. *platyanthum*.

GERANIUM FARRERI

Previously mis-named G. *napuligerum*, which is probably not in cultivation. Originating from western China, this is an enchanting little cranesbill 4–6in (10–15cm) high. It was introduced by Reginald Farrer in 1917 and has been beset by name changes over the years. It is a relief to know that it is back to G. *farreri* as an appropriate reminder of the discerning plantsman who discovered it. The flowers are exquisite ¾–1¼in (2–3cm), palest pink with conspicuous bluish-black anthers. It is best grown in a fairly rich scree mixture in the rock garden, trough or scree bed where it is well drained. As it disappears completely in winter, there are always anxious moments in spring, wondering if it will reappear. If not, it is easily raised from seed, or sometimes it is possible to separate the rosettes with tap root attached.

GERANIUM FAVOSUM

An annual originally from Africa, particularly Ethiopia. The stems are erect to about 10in (25cm), with finely cut leaves and strong pink flowers which have a black central eye. Quite often however, these flowers have a cleistogamous habit, in other words they form seeds through self-fertilisation without opening.

GERANIUM FREMONTII

From western North America, this is a large bushy plant, covered in sticky hairs and having numerous deeply divided leaves, coarsely lobed and toothed. The flowers are quite showy, 1½in (4cm), upwardly inclined and are borne on much-branched, rather flopping stems all summer. Thomas Hay in *Plants for the Connoisseur* (1938) described it thus: 'G. *fremontii* forms a fine rosette of long stalked and much divided deep green basal leaves from which arise many flower stems. The stem leaves are smaller, three to five cleft. The flowers are large and handsome, of a pleasing rose pink shade'. G. *fremontii* was tried in the rock garden but proved too big and untidy, and is more suited to a sunny place in the informal border. It needs frequent replanting, as the roots tend to work their way above the soil. Self-sown seedlings occasionally appear.

GERANIUM GLABERRIMUM

An alpine plant found at high altitudes in rock fissures, in the mountains of south-western Turkey. Growing to about 10in (25cm) in height, it has small kidney-shaped aromatic leaves and bright pink flowers 1in (2.5cm) with red anthers in summer. Although best suited to the alpine house, it might be worth trying outside in the rock garden. Propagate by seed.

GERANIUM GRACILE

Found in north-eastern Turkey and the Caucasus, this strongly resembles G. *nodosum* though it is taller 18–24in (45–60cm) and hairier. The leaves are similar in shape to those of G. *nodosum*, light green and wrinkled, having three large lobes and two smaller ones below, each finely serrated. The flowers are deeply funnel-shaped, with a white eye in the hollow, and notched petals which are distinctly marked with attractive short purple 'eye lash' veins. This is a geranium that prefers cooler woodland conditions, but performs quite well in the shade of shrubs, if not too dry. If propagated by division or seed it is worth selecting seedlings which show well-defined veining.

GERANIUM GYMNOCAULON

A native of north-eastern Turkey and the south-western Caucasus, G. *gymnocaulon* is a close relation of G. *ibericum*, though less vigorous and often short-lived. Growing to 12–18in (30–45cm) it has deeply cut, sharply toothed leaves and flattish flowers, 1³⁄₈in (3.5cm) in the height of summer. These are deep violet-blue with darker forked veins and notched petals. Grown in the border or large rock garden, G. *gymnocaulon* flowers better in full sun but is not averse to some shade. Divisions may tend to die out when replanted, so seed is the best bet for propagation.

GERANIUM HIMALAYENSE
(syn. G. *grandiflorum* and G. *meeboldii*)

A Himalayan species that spreads by underground rhizomes forming a dense carpet 12–18in (30–45cm) high. The handsome, finely-cut leaves colour brilliantly in autumn. Exception-

A neat-growing plant for the front of the border or alongside a path, G. *himalayense* 'Gravetye' has larger flowers than the type. They are rich violet blue with reddish accents and are displayed against finely-cut leaves

ally large saucer-shaped flowers 1¹⁄₂–2¹⁄₂in (4–6cm) across flutter above the foliage on thin stems and are a deep violet-blue flushed reddish-pink with a touch of white at the centre. G. *himalayense* starts to bloom in early summer and continues spasmodically into autumn. It makes excellent ground cover, stifling most weeds, but is also good at the front of the border and under shrubs – given room to expand. It is lovely with pale yellow and creamy roses, lavender, nepeta and the pale pink forms of G. × *oxonianum* – in fact practically anything! Regular division helps to keep the plants in good flowering form, and although it sets seed, it tends to hybridise with G. *pratense*, usually resulting in plants intermediate between the two.

G.h. 'Gravetye' is more compact, with even larger flowers and a more pronounced reddish centre.
G.h. 'Irish Blue', introduced from Eire by Mr Graham Thomas in 1947, is a vigorous plant that needs to be controlled. It has beautiful

paler blue flowers and an even larger reddish zone than G.h. 'Gravetye'. Very free flowering over a long period, its later flowers are particularly striking in association with the sumptuous *Cosmos atrosanguineus*, whose rich dark maroon, velvety blooms smell of hot chocolate. **G.h. 'Plenum'** (syn. G.h. 'Birch Double') is a pretty plant about 10–12in (25–30cm) in height, with small, round, divided leaves and charming double flowers 1in (2.5cm), of soft lilac, tinged with pinkish-violet. Although it is by no means as vigorous as the single forms (would that it were), it is worthy of a special place in the border in sun or half shade, where not too dry. The soft, woolly, silver foliage of *Stachys lanata* makes an ideal carpet for this delightful geranium, which although sterile can be propagated by division.

The hybrid G. 'Johnson's Blue' is very popular for its long season, the delicacy of its flowers and leaves, and its ability to fit into many different situations

GERANIUM IBERICUM subsp. IBERICUM

Originally from north-eastern Turkey and the Caucasus, this is a hairy plant about 18in (45cm) in height with handsome leaves, deeply divided into nine or eleven lobes, each divided again into numerous sharply toothed segments. Flowers 2in (5cm) are a good, deep violet-blue with dark feathered veins and notched petals. Its flowering season is rather brief – from early to mid-summer – although it may bloom again towards the end of summer. In the garden it is somewhat outshone by its more flamboyant cousin G. × *magnificum*, but it is useful in the sunny border under shrubs. To the layman's eye there seems to be hardly any difference between this and *G. ibericum* subsp. *jubatum*. It is best propagated by division or seed.

GERANIUM 'JOHNSON'S BLUE'
(G. himalayense × G. pratense)

Named after A.T. Johnson, from one of whose hybrid seedlings this particular form was selected. A splendid and deservedly popular plant, making dense clumps of finely cut foliage 12–18in (30–45cm). Copious lavender-blue flowers 2in (5cm) flushed with reddish pink are produced from mid-summer to autumn. Easily grown in sun or shade, it makes excellent ground cover and an ideal partner for pale yellow and creamy coloured roses. G. 'Johnson's Blue' is sterile, but its underground rhizomes provide plenty of material for propagation.

G. 'Joy', see page 76 for a list of Alan Bremner's hybrids.

GERANIUM 'KASHMIR BLUE'
(G. pratense albiflorum × G. clarkei 'Kashmir White')

G. 'Kashmir Blue' was raised by Ivan Louette in Belgium in the mid-1980s. Although the name suggests a cultivar of *G. clarkei*, G. 'Kashmir Blue' resembles *G. pratense* in size and foliage, but has very large flowers of a soft pale blue from early to mid-summer. Further confusion arises as 'Kashmir Purple' is sometimes distributed as 'Kashmir Blue'.

GERANIUM 'KATE'
(G. endressii × G. sessiliflorum)

G. 'Kate' was discovered by the Rev Oliver Folkard in his Lincolnshire garden, the hybrid being named after his daughter. It is sometimes referred to as 'Kate Folkard'. A dwarf plant 4–6in (10–15cm) in height, its leaves resemble those of *G. sessiliflorum* 'Nigricans'. The flowers ³⁄₈–³⁄₄in (1–2cm) are funnel-shaped, pale pink with a translucent white centre with darker

veins, through which the green, brown-tinged sepals are visible. 'Kate' is sterile, but can be propagated by division.

GERANIUM KERBERI

Originally from Mexico, *G. kerberi* is a tall, flopping geranium up to 40in (1m), with palmate leaves. Its flowers ¹⁄₂in (1.5cm) are white or pale lilac, with strong, dark veins and notched petals. It is not hardy where I live in Somerset.

GERANIUM KISHTVARIENSE

This species from Kashmir was introduced by Roy Lancaster in 1978. It is a bushy plant spreading by thin underground stolons. The basal leaves are deeply divided into five broad, sharply toothed lobes, rather light green in colour and wrinkled on the surface. The upper leaves are three-lobed. The flowers 1¹⁄₂in (4cm), produced all summer and into autumn, are an intensely bright pinkish-purple with fine purple veins, a small white eye and blackish-red stamens. The plant prefers shade or partial shade in woodland conditions where the soil retains some moisture. It can be propagated by division or seed.

GERANIUM KRAMERI

A native of northern China, Korea and Japan, *G. krameri* has distinctive leaves, very deeply cut into long, narrow, coarsely serrated segments. Stems, up to 31in (80cm), are usually floppy. Flowers are about ³⁄₄in (2cm), pale pink with darker veins. *G. krameri* has no real garden value and is best confined to the wild or woodland garden in light shade. It is propagated by seed.

GERANIUM LAMBERTII
(syn. G. grevilleanum)

A sprawling Himalayan plant producing most foliage on the flower stems and building up to quite substantial mounds 12–18in (30–45cm). Its leaves are rather soft and wrinkled, and are a rich green with deeply toothed lobes. The flowers are amongst the most beautiful of all hardy geraniums, 1 1/4–1 1/2in (3–4cm) – saucer-shaped, shyly nodding pale pink, usually with a central crimson stain and further enhanced by black anthers. The flowering season is from mid-summer into autumn. It is seen to best advantage on a raised bed or bank or where the trailing stems can intertwine with low-growing shrubs in partial shade. It may be propagated by seed.

G.l. 'Swansdown', sometimes mistakenly called *G. candidum* or *G. candicans*. The gorgeous white flowers have pale veins, a pronounced crimson centrepiece and black anthers. Bright green sepals are visible between the petals, and the leaves are marbled with two shades of green. It comes true when propagated by seed.

GERANIUM LANUGINOSUM

From the Mediterranean region and Sweden, this annual is very similar to *G. bohemicum*. A sprawling, hairy plant growing from a rosette of deeply cut and marbled leaves with narrower segments than *G. bohemicum*, and unwrinkled. Flowers 1/2in (1.5cm), campanula-blue with a pale pinkish-white centre. It is not really garden-worthy.

GERANIUM LIBANI
(syn. *Geranium libanoticum*)

This distinctive geranium comes from Lebanon, western Syria, and central and southern Turkey. The handsome leaves, which appear in autumn, are glossy on the upper surface with paler veins, and rather widely spaced gaps between the divisions and lobes. The flowers 1 1/2in (4cm) wide are borne in spring; they are an attractive violet-blue with notched petals and slightly feathered veins. They stand well above the foliage. The whole plant dies down after flowering, often leaving dense mats of thick roots exposed, which

A part-time geranium that becomes dormant after its spring flowering, reviving again in the autumn, *G. libani* has slightly cupped violet-blue flowers and attractive leaves

need replanting or mulching. *G. libani* is well-behaved enough to include in the rock garden or at the front of the border, but needs later-flowering companions to fill the gap when it is dormant. Propagate from seed, or by dividing the roots.

GERANIUM × LINDAVICUM

G. × lindavicum is the name given by Dr Yeo to crosses between *G. argenteum* and *G. cinereum*. These include some desirable plants for the rock garden, trough or scree in well-drained, gritty soil in full sun. They all dislike winter wet, which causes the crowns to rot, but covering with a pane of glass during the winter months will alleviate the problem. Propagation is by stem or root cuttings.

G. × l. 'Alanah' is described by Walter Ingwersen in *The Genus Geranium* (1946) as 'a very attractive plant but slightly less silvery in foliage than *G. argenteum* and extremely free in the production of its vivid crimson-purple flowers. It is shy to increase'. He considered it to be the same plant as *G. argenteum purpureum* (*G. × lindavicum* 'Purpureum').

G. × l. 'Apple Blossom' (syn. 'Jenny Bloom'): G. × l. 'Apple Blossom' was raised by Bloom's Nursery in Norfolk. It is low growing, 6in (15cm) with neat tufts of deeply-cut, silvery leaves, the divisions cut again into three lobes. Lovely, lightly veined flowers of palest pink are borne in summer.

G. × l. 'Gypsy': it is doubtful if this most attractive cross, raised by Eric Smith in Dorset, is still in the land of the living. I hope to be proved wrong in stating that the flamboyant, aptly named 'Gypsy' was lost by all who grew her, in the hard winter of 1984. Somewhat taller than the other forms of *G. lindavicum* mentioned, its greyish-green leaves are deeply cut and sharply toothed. The rounded flowers are unique in colour, well described by Dr Yeo as 'a brilliant pink-cerise shot with carmine, fading to white just above the maroon, butterfly-shaped blotch at the base, and closely net-veined with maroon; the anthers are black and the filaments and stigmas much the same colour as the petal-blotch'.

G. × l. 'Lissadell': a beautiful little plant which forms compact hummocks of small, finely cut, silvery-green foliage topped with deep plum-coloured flowers. Cuttings are difficult to root.

The flowers of G. x *lindavicum* 'Lissadell' glow like jewels against the bright silvery leaves

GERANIUM MACRORRHIZUM

Originating in the mountainous areas of southern Europe and often naturalising elsewhere in Europe, *G. macrorrhizum* is one of the best ground-cover plants, spreading by fleshy underground rhizomes and thick rooting stems, making dense mats 12–18in (30–45cm) across in sun, but tolerant of dry shade. The rounded, broadly lobed leaves are sticky and aromatic. Their scent, to me, is of sweetbrier, but not everyone would agree. Some leaves are retained in winter, especially in milder areas and often assume rich autumn tints. Clusters of flowers 1in (2.5cm) are borne in early summer. They are a rather dull magenta, a colour that is not altogether compatible with the reddish-brown sepals which form a bladder-like calyx. Propagation is simple, from detached pieces of rhizome.

G. m. 'Album', introduced by Walter Ingwersen from Bulgaria, is a lovely white-flowered form with a faint flush of pink. Calyces and stamens are also pink.

G. m. 'Bevan's Variety' has flowers of a deep magenta with clashing red sepals.

G. m. 'Czakor' is an improvement on the above, with deep magenta-pink flowers.

G. m. 'Ingwersen's Variety' is one of the best, having lighter green foliage and pretty soft pink flowers.

G. m. 'Lohfelden' is a recent introduction from Germany. It is of shorter stature, resembling G. × *cantabrigiense*. The flowers are flushed a pale pink, veined a deeper pink.

G. m. 'Ridsko' has smooth, rather glossy deciduous leaves with magenta-pink flowers.

G. m. 'Spessart': a pink-flowered form is often sold under this name, but the true plant originated as a white-flowered seedling raised by Dr Hans Simon, one which is very similar to *G.m.* 'Album'.

G. m. 'Variegatum' is a good foliage plant when well grown. It has greyish-green leaves, irregularly splashed with deep cream and flowers that are a purplish-pink. Unfortunately it is not so vigorous as the plain-leaved forms, needing a rich diet, more moisture and preferably a little sun.

GERANIUM MACROSTYLUM

A pretty little cranesbill from Greece, Albania, southern Yugoslavia and central and western Turkey, *G. macrostylum* spreads rapidly by small tubers. The leaves are deeply and finely cut into five or seven narrow segments, each deeply toothed, giving a feathery appearance. Slender stems up to 15in (38cm) bear rather frail flowers 1in (2.5cm), which are pale mauvish-pink with faint darker veins, and deeply notched petals. There is also a lavender-blue form. The plants become dormant after flowering in early summer, reappearing the following spring. The small tubers are often dispersed by cats, or during weeding, and can become a nuisance in the rock garden, so it is perhaps advisable to grow it in paving or containers. The tubers present plenty of material for propagation.

The rosy magenta flowers of G. *macrorrhizum* 'Bevan's Variety' produce an especially opulent effect en masse, and with its enduring aromatic foliage, the plant gives continuing interest

GERANIUM MACULATUM

An erect cranesbill originally from eastern North America, G. *maculatum* grows up to 28in (70cm), from a stout rootstock. The handsome, fairly large leaves are deeply divided into five or seven rather widely spaced lobes, the divisions being sharply toothed. The name 'maculatum' implies spotting but this is not apparent on cultivated plants. Descriptions in *Floras* of plants native to North America refer to 'faint spots on the leaves'. Shallow, bowl-shaped flowers 1 1/4in (3cm) are pale to deep pink in colour, white at the centre with greyish-blue anthers. They are borne in clusters in late spring, summer and often again in autumn. Inhabiting rich, moist woodlands and meadows in the wild, G. *maculatum* performs better in the garden if the soil is dampish. A useful addition to the spring border, stream side or wild garden in sun or part shade. It is propagated by division or seed, and is often self-sowing.

G.m. 'Album' is a lovely white form, but not easy to please, especially in drought conditions.

GERANIUM MADERENSE

A dramatic plant originating from Madeira, this is like a giant Herb Robert, growing from an impressive rosette, raised on a distinct stem which is almost a trunk. The leaves, which are the largest of any of the species, are aromatic and much divided on brownish-red stems. When the flowers are massed above the foliage, it will reach 40in (1m) or more. Flowering starts in late winter or early spring and each bloom measures 1 1/2in (4cm) across. The purplish-pink flowers are overlaid with pale, netted veins and have dark crimson centres and dark red anthers. G. *maderense* is not hardy except in very mild, sheltered areas, but makes a stunning pot plant if given winter protection in the greenhouse. Plants may die after flowering, but sometimes grow on from side shoots. It can be propagated by seed, after storing for a month or so. Young plants need frequent repotting to prevent their growth being checked.

GERANIUM × MAGNIFICUM
(G. *ibericum* × G. *platypetalum*)

A vigorous sterile hybrid, established in gardens for over a hundred years. It is superior to both its parents, but often sold under either of their names. Rounded, hairy leaves are divided into rather broad segments, taking on pleasing shades in autumn. It spreads steadily, making broad clumps 20–28in (50–70cm) in height. The saucer-shaped flowers 2in (5cm) are a striking rich violet, darkly veined and produced in abundance over a comparatively short period in midsummer. It is magnificent in the border, in sun or part shade, with *Iris pallida*, blue grasses and the pale yellow achilleas. It also makes excellent ground cover under yellow or pink roses, golden foliage shrubs and with blue-leaved hostas. Propagation is by division.

GERANIUM MALVIFLORUM

In the past, this geranium from southern Spain and Morocco was mis-named G. *atlanticum*. Growing to about 12in (30cm) and spreading rapidly by knobbly tubers, it has the largest leaves of all the tuberous-rooted cranesbills. These are divided to the base into feathered divisions, dying down after flowering, and usually re-emerging in autumn, providing attractive winter foliage. The large 1 1/2in (4cm) saucer-shaped flowers appear suddenly in early spring and are violet-blue with strong, darker veins. In some years it refuses to bloom at all, but in full sun and poor soil, especially if contained in paving, results are much better. There is a clone which does not reappear until spring, and has slightly larger flowers with a pink tinge. It also flowers more freely. Propagation is achieved by dividing the numerous tubers.

GERANIUM 'MARY MOTTRAM'

This plant was originally purchased from the late Mary Mottram's nursery in Devon, by Joan and Robin Grout of Nottingham, as G. *endressii album*. However, it turned out to be such a

The strongly reflexed flowers of G. × *monacense* nothovar.
anglicum show off the various coloured zones in their centres

120

superior plant that they thought it might be a hybrid. Dr Yeo has now confirmed that it is a cross between *G. endressii* and *G. sylvaticum* 'Album'. It has a very neat habit, growing to about 12in (30cm) tall. The pure white flowers continue all summer and repeat in autumn if deadheaded. The name 'Mary Mottram' has been approved.

GERANIUM MASCATENSE

An annual from Africa, *G. mascatense* has a wide distribution, growing up to 12in (30cm) in height, with deeply cut leaves, and flowers similar to those of *G. ocellatum* – deep vivid pink with a black centre. It is quite attractive for the odd corner of the garden in sun, often producing self-sown seedlings.

GERANIUM × MONACENSE
(*G. phaeum* × *G. reflexum* syn. *G. punctatum* of gardens)

A garden hybrid with characteristics midway between its parents. The leaves are usually

Geranium × monacense

blotched with brown, often turning a clear primrose-yellow in autumn. Flowers are a dull purplish-pink with a central white zone edged and veined with violet and the petals strongly reflexed. A useful plant for shade. It can be propagated by division.

G. × m. nothovar *anglicum* (*G. phaeum lividum* × *G. reflexum*) has flowers of pale lilac-pink, a small central zone, with a wide bluish-violet edging, strongly veined.

G. × m. 'Eric Clement' is a more vigorous plant with slightly larger flowers with the petals curving forward at the tips.

G. × m. 'Muldoon' is a striking clone which has very bold purplish-brown blotching on the leaves. Unfortunately the name is sometimes misapplied to *G. phaeum* 'Variegatum'.

GERANIUM NEPALENSE

Originally from eastern Afghanistan, the Himalayas and China, this is a weedy species with dark green marbled leaves, that are often purple on the underside. The flowers are small, only $\frac{3}{8}$in (1cm) across, white, pale or deep pink with darker veins and are carried on thin trailing stems. *G. nepalense* has no real garden value except perhaps to the ardent collector.

GERANIUM NERVOSUM
(syn. *G. strigosum*)

From western North America and sometimes sold as *G. incisum*. It is a very variable plant, similar to *G. viscosissimum* with the same sticky-haired characteristics. Light green aromatic leaves are broadly lobed with sharply toothed divisions. Flat flowers $\frac{3}{4}$ to $1\frac{1}{2}$in (2–4cm) across are usually borne from early summer onwards on a single stem which branches at the

G. nervosum is a native of western North America and deserves to be more widely known. The flower colour can be variable, but this rich pink form with contrasting veining is very distinctive

top. Flower colour is pink to purplish-red with darker veins and a small white centre. *G. nervosum* is attractive enough for a position in the sunny border and can grow 12–18in (30–45cm) tall, though it may vary somewhat in height. It will also grow in quite dry shade under trees and shrubs. It can be propagated by division (which needs care) or by seed.

GERANIUM 'NIMBUS'
(*G. collinum* × G. 'Kashmir Purple')

This hybrid occurred at Cambridge University Botanic Garden in 1978 and was introduced by Axletree Nursery in 1990. It has very finely cut, feathery leaves, gold-tinged when young. The flowers 1in (2.5cm) are purplish-pink with darker veins and a small white centre. The rather widely spaced petals give the flowers a most appealing countenance. Propagation is by division.

Geranium nodosum

GERANIUM NODOSUM

Originally found in the mountains of southern France, central Italy and central Yugoslavia, this is an enchanting cranesbill for woodland or a shady border; colonising under trees in dry, quite dense shade, it forms spreading clumps of most attractive foliage. The leaves are bright green and glossy, divided into three or five lobes and finely serrated. The funnel-shaped flowers 1–1 1/4in (2.5–3cm) are bright lilac-pink or pink, with deeply notched, lightly veined petals. Some gardeners complain that it self-sows too freely, but never enough in my garden. Propagation is by division of the slender underground rhizomes, or by seed.

G. 'Nora Bremner', see page 76 for a list of Alan Bremner's hybrids.

GERANIUM OCELLATUM

A native of the mountains of western and eastern Africa, the Arabian Peninsula, the Himalayas and south-western China. This annual is prostrate in habit, with thin, spreading stems up to 28in (70cm) and rounded leaves divided into five- or seven-toothed lobes. Flowers 3/8in (1cm) are a vivid purplish-pink with a black eye, often not opening (cleistogamous). *G. ocellatum* is of little garden value, although the flowers are attractive if they open. It self-sows mildly.

GERANIUM OREGANUM

From western North America, *G. oreganum* is a lovely plant with leaves similar to those of *G. pratense*, forming compact clumps 24in (60cm) high, and twice as wide. Upward-facing, saucer-shaped flowers about 2in (5cm) are a deep rose-pink and abundant in mid-summer. It makes a good border plant, weaving through its neighbours, although according to the late Dennis Thompson, of Seattle, USA, 'it seems most at home on steep slopes under high shrubs or mingling with grasses'. It is propagated by division or seed.

GERANIUM ORIENTALITIBETICUM

A native of south-western China and previously known to gardeners as *G. stapfianum roseum*. This pretty little species 8in (20cm) high, runs about energetically by strings of small underground tubers. It is worth growing for its deeply cut, rounded, light green leaves which are strongly marbled with yellow or pale cream. The flattish flowers 1in (2.5cm) are deep pink with a large white central zone. It is rather too invasive for the smaller rock garden and is best grown at the edge of the border or in paving or containers, in sun and well-drained soil. Propagate by lifting and dividing the tubers.

GERANIUM × OXONIANUM

This is the name given by Dr Yeo to hybrids between *G. endressii* and *G. versicolor*. They are all fertile as far as I know, except 'Southcombe Double' and 'Southcombe Star'. They make excellent garden plants for a variety of situations in sun or shade, especially for dense, weed-smothering ground cover. All benefit from severe shearing to the ground after the main flush of flowers.

G. × o. 'A.T. Johnson' syn. 'Johnson's Variety' raised by A.T. Johnson in North Wales pre-1937. It has similar leaves to *G. endressii*, but is shorter in stature, covering itself in masses of light silvery-pink translucent flowers all the summer. It is particularly lovely with mauves and purples.

G. × o. 'Claridge Druce' was raised by Dr Claridge Druce around 1900. It is a very vigorous plant developing into massive mounds of dark greyish-green, glossy, evergreen foliage up to 24in (60cm) or more – guaranteed to smother anything in its path. The large trumpet-shaped flowers are deep rosy-pink with a strong network of darker veins. Given the right situation with plenty of space, it makes marvellous ground cover for large areas where there is no danger of other plants being overlaid. There are always plenty of self-sown seedlings which are likely to vary considerably.

G. × o. 'Hollywood' is a recent introduction from Langthorns Plantery and is similar to 'Claridge Druce' but with smaller, lighter green leaves. The large flowers 1½in (4cm) are pale pink with strongly netted magenta veins and overlapping petals.

G. × o. 'Lady Moore' is another strong-growing plant of the 'Claridge Druce' persuasion, having splendid blotched foliage and large darkly-veined flowers on a background of deep pinkish-purple.

G. × o. 'Rose Clair'. The true plant as grown in the National Collection at Cherry Hinton Hall, Cambridge, is a long flowering form with glowing rosy pink flowers which have faint veining, but forms of *G. versicolor* are often listed erroneously under this name.

G × o. 'Sherwood' is an introduction from Axletree Nursery (1991). Resembling *G. × o.* 'Thurstonianum', which is very variable, *G. × 'Sherwood'* has narrower pale pink petals and sometimes petaloid stamens, which give the appearance of extra petals.

A strong-growing form of *G. x oxonianum*, *G. x o.* 'Lady Moore' has a summer-long display of mid-pink flowers, laced with darker veins. The intriguing story of its origin is described on page 19

124

G. × o. 'Southcombe Double' is from South-combe Garden Plant Nursery (1982) and is shorter and less vigorous than the typical G. × *oxonianum* – about 15in (38cm) tall. The flowers are small ³⁄₄in (2cm), deep salmon-pink, often with petaloid stamens, giving a double-flowered effect. Plants tend to die out in the middle of the clumps, and benefit from occasional replanting.

G. × o. 'Southcombe Star', again from South-combe Garden Plant Nursery (1983), and very similar to 'Southcombe Double' but less compact. The flowers are star-like in appearance and bluish-pink with narrow petals.

G. × o. 'Thurstonianum' is an oddity, making a large plant up to 24in (60cm) or more. The dark green foliage is sometimes blotched with purplish-brown. The aberrant flowers have very narrow, often twisted petals of bright reddish-purple, white at the base and deeply notched. This variety sometimes produces petaloid stamens, resulting in semi-double flowers. Its progeny are very varied, and you are liable to acquire any of them under the name 'Thurstonianum'.

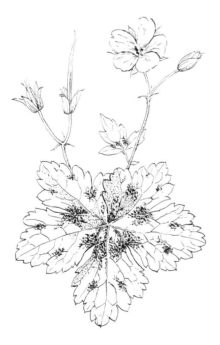

Geranium × oxonianum 'Walter's Gift'

G. × o. 'Walter's Gift' is named after the former home of Mary Ramsdale in Essex, where this seedling occurred. About 24in (61cm) in height, it has shiny green leaves with a dark reddish suffusion spreading out from the centre, the area of colour being variable. The flowers are small, pale pink with a network of magenta veins.

G. × o. 'Winscombe' was discovered by Margery Fish in a Somerset garden. It is similar in habit to G. *endressii*, but the flowers open a very pale silvery-pink, then change to deeper pink as they mature, giving a delightful two-tone effect on the one plant.

G. 'Pagoda', see page 76 for a list of Alan Bremner's hybrids.

GERANIUM PALMATUM
(syn. G. *anemonifolium*)

Originally from Madeira, G. *palmatum* resembles, and is often confused with, G. *canariense*, but G. *palmatum* has hardly any rosette stem on young plants, and the leaves are larger with green or pink-flushed stems up to 48in (122cm) in height. The flowers, borne in great profusion in summer, 1¹⁄₄–1¹⁄₂in (3–4cm) are purplish-pink with a deep crimson central zone. Though not reliably hardy, it may survive outside in sheltered corners on dry soil, and makes a very showy pot-plant for the greenhouse.

G. *palmatum* has a life-span of about three years, after which the main growth usually ceases, but it often produces fresh rosettes from the base. It is so easily raised from seed that it is really better at this stage to start again with new plants.

GERANIUM PALUSTRE

Originally from eastern and central Europe, G. *palustre* inhabits damp places in the wild; however, it is very drought-resistant in the garden. It forms low-growing, bushy hummocks of fresh green, deeply cut leaves which are coarsely and rather sparsely toothed. Thin stems radiate from the central rootstock up to 16in (40cm). The trumpet-shaped flowers 1¹⁄₄in (3cm) are bright magenta-pink, veined dark purple with a small white eye and violet anthers. The long flowering period from early summer into autumn makes it a useful plant for filling gaps in the border where it can weave its way through neighbours that have ceased to bloom. It can be divided, and usually self-sows quite liberally.

GERANIUM PAPUANUM

A creeping, mat-forming species introduced from the high mountains of Papua New Guinea by the Rev Norman Cruttwell. It resembles a miniature *G. sanguineum* with small, rounded, deeply dissected, shiny leaves, dark green in colour. Flowers, which are poised on short stems just above the foliage, are a bright rose colour with darker veins. *G. papuanum* may prove difficult to keep in the open garden in the UK. It is probably frost tender but would make an attractive plant for the alpine house, shaded from the midday sun. It is easy to propagate from pieces of the rooting stems. Seed is rather sparse and not easy to collect.

G. 'Patricia', see page 77 for a list of Alan Bremner's hybrids.

GERANIUM PELOPONNESIACUM

Originally from Greece, *G. peloponnesiacum* was introduced to cultivation by Richard Gorer in 1972. This species has great charm. Growing from a thick rhizome to about 24in (60cm) though often less, it has pretty, rather wrinkled velvety leaves, similar to those of *G. renardii*, though less rounded in outline and the divisions are diamond-shaped. The leaves die down after flowering has taken place, reappearing in autumn. The flowers are carried in clusters on tall stems in late spring. They are funnel-shaped, 1½in (4cm) and slatey violet-blue in colour, with dark feathery veins and deeply notched petals. *G. peloponnesiacum* is a dainty plant that could be grown in the rock garden or border, in sun or part shade. It can be propagated by division or seed, though this is not freely set.

GERANIUM PHAEUM

From the mountains of southern and central Europe, this was voted the most popular cranesbill in 1991 by members of the Hardy Plant Society's Hardy Geranium Group, chiefly for its ability to grow in deep, dry shade. It has been nicknamed 'The Mourning Widow' on account of its unusually dark, sombre nodding flowers and not, as sometimes imagined, because it only flowers in the morning! It is also known as 'The Dusky Cranesbill'. A strong-growing plant, up to 31in (80cm), it makes generous clumps of leaves, rather shallowly divided into seven or nine profusely toothed lobes. The leaves and stems are sometimes spotted with purplish-brown. The flattish flowers are very dark maroon, nearly black, with a little point at the tip of each petal and a small white central area. There are several variants which, when grown together, will hybridise among themselves, resulting in all kinds of intermediate shades. The dark forms are set off to best advantage against a light background, such as shrubs with silver or golden foliage. All *G. phaeum* make excellent ground cover and can be divided easily as a means of propagation. Seed, though, will be variable.

G. p. 'Album' is a lovely clear white with large flowers, made even more attractive by golden anthers.

G. p. 'Lily Lovell' was raised and introduced by Trevor Bath of Mayford, Surrey, and named after his mother. The large flowers, a beautifully rich mauve, are set off well by the distinctive light green foliage.

G. p. var. *lividum* is a pretty form with pale greyish-lilac flowers.

G. p. var. l. 'Joan Baker' occurred in the garden of A.W.A. (Bill) Baker, near Pangbourne in Berkshire, and is named after his wife. A strong grower 36in (91cm) in height, it has very pale lavender flowers 1in (2.5cm) with a distinctive darker ring near the centre.

G. p. var. l. 'Majus' is taller than the usual lividum form, with larger flowers.

An improved form of G. *phaeum*, G.*p.* 'Lily Lovell' has larger flowers of rich mauve with paler centres. It was raised and introduced by Trevor Bath, and is named in memory of his mother

G. p. 'Samobor', a variety recently introduced by Washfield Nursery. It has typical G. *phaeum* flowers, but the large leaves are arrestingly zoned with dark brown. Wonderful for foliage effect.

G. p. 'Taff's Jester' was discovered by Stephen Taffler in a garden in the Home Counties. The whole or part of each leaf is mottled with rich yellow, irregularly splashed with yellowish-green, and blotched with purplish-brown in the notches. The flowers are dark, like those of the typical G. *phaeum*.

G. p. 'Variegatum' has leaves splashed with cream and pale green, and the occasional bright reddish-pink streaks or spots.

G. 'Philippe Vapelle', see page 77 for a list of Alan Bremner's hybrids.

GERANIUM PLATYANTHUM
(syn. *G. eriostemon*)

Originally found in north-eastern Asia, eastern Tibet, western China, Korea and Japan, this is an interesting, hairy geranium growing from a thick rootstock with upright stems to about 24in (60cm). The large, light green leaves are cut to about halfway into broad, shallowly lobed and toothed divisions. It has been somewhat maligned by being described as having 'muddy' flowers, but in fact these are not by any means unattractive. They are held in dense clusters from late spring to early summer, are rather flat $1\frac{1}{4}$in (3cm), and slatey mauve-pink with a white centre. G. *platyanthum* can be grown in sun or half shade, in the wild or woodland garden, and also makes an unusual addition to the spring border, often flowering again towards autumn. It is easily propagated by division or seed.

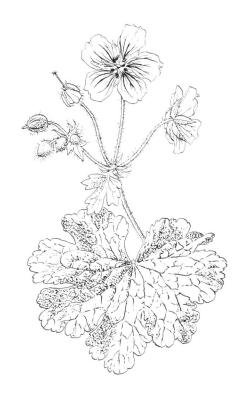

Geranium platypetalum

GERANIUM PLATYPETALUM

Another hairy plant, this time from the Caucasus. It is similar to *G. ibericum*, growing from a thick rootstock, but the wrinkled leaves are not so deeply cut, being broader lobed and less sharply toothed. The stems reach 12–18in (30–45cm) from compact clumps. Shallow saucer-shaped flowers 1¼–1½in (3–4cm) are a good deep violet-blue, paler at the centre with prominent dark, forking veins, notched petals and bluish-black anthers. The flowering season is usually mid-summer, but often repeats again later. *G. platypetalum* is lovely with pale pink or yellow roses in sun or part shade. Blue grasses, ballota, *Sisyrinchium striatum* (now *Phaiophleps nigricans*) and *Alchemilla mollis* also make pleasing associates. It is propagated by division or seed.

GERANIUM POGONANTHUM

From south-western China and western and northern Burma, *G. pogonanthum* was introduced to cultivation by Frank Kingdon-Ward in 1956 and originally distributed as *G. yunnanense*. *G. pogonanthum* is attractive in both leaf and flower, growing from a compact, stout rootstock to a height of 18–24in (45–60cm). The deeply lobed, sharply toothed leaves are marbled with yellowish-green. Its distinctively beautiful nodding flowers on lax stems are a dusky pink with narrow reflexed petals, like miniature cyclamen, and black anthers. It needs careful placing, as the delicate beauty of the flowers can be swamped by robust neighbours. A lightly shaded corner where the geranium stems could weave through grey or purple foliage would suit it well. It needs replanting when the roots work their way above the soil; it can be propagated by division or seed.

GERANIUM POLYANTHES

From the Himalayas and south-western China, *G. polyanthes* grows from knobbly, reddish-brown, tuber-like roots which constantly push their way above soil, needing replanting or mulching. The leaves are small, shiny, succulent and kidney-shaped. Funnel-shaped flowers 1in (2.5cm) are produced in summer and are bright, shiny pink with finely pencilled veins, held in clusters on stems up to 18in (45cm) but usually only about 8in (20cm). *G. polyanthes* is refined enough for the rock garden or front of the border, the new growth appearing so late that one fears the worst. Sometimes those fears are justified, for in my experience it has a habit of dying out after three or four years. However, it is easily divided or raised from seed.

GERANIUM POTENTILLOIDES

A native of Australia and New Zealand. Seed of this species is sometimes offered by specialist societies. It grows from a deep tap root, producing small white flowers, occasionally pink, ⅜in (1cm) on weak, straggling stems.

GERANIUM PRATENSE

The typical Meadow Cranesbill from northern Europe and Asia, as described in the British Natives section (p142). While the wild form itself should not be despised in the garden, especially for naturalising in rough grass, there are a number of superior garden forms. The trouble is that all are prolific seeders, except for the double forms, which are sterile. Unless you have unlimited space to accommodate their offspring, it is advisable to snip off the seedheads before they mature, or cut the whole plant to the ground when the flowers are past their best. It will grow and bloom again. Inevitably some seed will escape but at least the seedlings will be more controllable. *G. pratense* makes very substantial clumps with strong, fleshy roots which can be quite a job to divide, but this is the best method of propagation as seed will be variable.

G. p. **forma albiflorum** is the name given to white-flowered variants, both in the wild and cultivation. The best of these are a lovely clear white.

128

G. p. **'Bittersweet'** is a recent introduction which has pale mauve-pink flowers with paler veins and dark anthers in early summer. The foliage is tinged with purple.

G. p. **'Galactic'** is the name given by Dr Yeo to a shorter, sturdier plant with a flatter flowerhead. The name suggests the milky whiteness of its overlapping petals – a lovely form.

G. p. **'Mrs Kendall Clark'.** The original plant of this name was said by Walter Ingwersen to be 'pearl grey flushed with softest rose'. The one sent to the Wisley Trials in 1976 by Bloom's Nurseries was of the violet-blue group with white veining, and this is the plant which is generally distributed as 'Mrs Kendall Clark' nowadays. It is very lovely in its own right, and very much admired, standing some 24–36in (60–90cm) or more. Seedlings result in a diversity of different markings, some heavily veined, some with two distinct oval blotches near the tip of each petal, others with random blotches, all on a pale grey-blue background (I suspect a liason with *G.p.* 'Striatum'). The flopping stems when in full flower need support from more substantial neighbours. In a border where tidiness is not paramount, a glorious tangle can be achieved with 'Mrs Kendall Clark', *Anthemis tinctoria* 'E.C. Buxton' and *Geranium psilostemon* intermingling.

G. p. **'Silver Queen'** was raised by A.T. Johnson and is a stately, strong grower. Another case of the original plant, which was said to have 'large silver-blue flowers', being virtually replaced by one with 'white with a slight tinge of very pale violet, particularly when young' (Wisley Trial Report 1976). The latter is the one generally seen these days as 'Silver Queen', tall and lovely, often with prominent black anthers.

G. p. **'Striatum'** (syn. *G.p.* 'Bicolor') is an attractive and very intriguing variant with basically white petals, irregularly splashed, streaked or just spotted with clear violet-blue. The degree of colouring varies greatly on the same plant – sometimes a whole or half petal is blue and

Geranium pratense

others only slightly speckled. The cause of this phenomenon is, apparently, an unstable gene which mutates during the plant's growth.

G. pratense – double forms. There are three double forms of G. *pratense*, all desirable and all sterile. They have that 'old world' charm which looks so right in the cottage garden, but they are equally at home in the grand borders of large estates.

G. p. 'Plenum Album' has loosely petalled white rosettes tinged with violet which gives a slightly greyish appearance that is nevertheless very charming. It is not as robust as the other two double forms of G. *pratense*; it needs pampering in good rich soil, and careful division from time to time to keep it in good condition.

G. p. 'Plenum Caeruleum' is a splendid 'old-fashioned' geranium, smothering itself in early summer in quantities of small lavender-blue rosettes tinged with pink. Silver or grey foliage plants such as *Phlomis viscosa* make an ideal foil for the lavender flowers. Regular division is needed as large clumps become unweildy and prone to mildew, particularly in dry conditions.

An intriguingly eccentric version of G. *pratense*, G.*p.* 'Striatum' (formerly G.*p.* 'Bicolor') is basically a white-flowered form, in which individual flowers are variably marked and streaked with blue, ranging from dots and dashes to whole blue petals

The plant should be cut right down after flowering to induce new growth and perhaps more flowers.

G. p. 'Plenum Violaceum' (G.*p.* 'Purpureum Plenum') blooms later than G.*p.* 'Plenum Caeruleum', extending the season over a long period. Perfectly formed pompoms of rich violet with darker centres begin flowering in mid-summer. It is especially delightful when mingling with *Linaria purpurea* 'Canon J. Went' and silver foliage or, for a stronger theme, orange lilies or roses.

GERANIUM PROCURRENS

A Himalayan geranium, a low, rampant ground-cover plant. It spreads rapidly by long, thin, reddish stems which root busily at the nodes, forming new plants as they travel, and covering a

130

large area in one season. Light green, wrinkled and lightly mottled leaves are elegantly cut into tapered lobes. The flowers are a rather sombre pinkish-purple 1in (2.5cm) across, with dark centres and black veins and bloom from mid-summer into autumn. G. *procurrens* is really too vigorous for a small garden unless the stems can be persuaded to grow upwards through shrubs, where they are unable to contact the soil. In our small garden, the problem has been overcome by planting it on the outside of the front hedge, where it weaves its way through to the top

Geranium procurrens

and enlivens the *Lonicera nitida* with its flowers. Large areas under trees or a specimen tree or shrub can be covered effectively in a short time. As the connecting stems die away in winter, leaving the rooted youngsters in situ, the spaces in between could be planted with early flowering bulbs. The rooted plantlets provide a plentiful source for new stock. Hybrids from G. *procurrens* include G. 'Ann Folkard', G. 'Anne Thomson' and G. 'Dilys' which are all too ladylike to be rampant.

GERANIUM PSEUDOSIBIRICUM
(G. *sylvaticum* subsp. *pseudosibiricum*)

Originally from the Ural Mountains and Siberia. It resembles G. *rivulare* although the leaves are smaller and the blue or lilac flowers only ½in (1.5cm). It is not thought to be in cultivation in the UK but is mentioned here as the name is sometimes mistakenly applied to the Siberian forms of G. *pratense*.

GERANIUM PSILOSTEMON
(syn G. *armenum*)

A native of north-eastern Turkey and the south-western Caucasus, this is a spectacular cranesbill for the border which can reach 48in (122cm) in sun or light shade. It has very large, deeply cut and sharply toothed leaves which turn brilliant flame-red in autumn. The bowl-shaped flowers 1½in (4cm), in sizzling magenta with a black centre and black veins, make a wonderful display all through summer. Such is the intensity of the colour that some visitors to the garden have been known to recoil in horror, whilst others find it fascinating. Combining it with pale yellow or pink flowers, silver foliage and the pale blue forms of G. *pratense*, will help to cool down the strong magenta. Intrepid gardeners may prefer to make it even hotter by planting *Geranium psilostemon* among strong yellow, orange and purple.

G.p. 'Bressingham Flair' was introduced by Bloom's Nurseries in 1973, though this hybrid is not quite so tall as the original species, and much softer in colour. It is a nice plant but lacks the impact of its showier cousin. Both can be propagated by division or seed.

GERANIUM PYLZOWIANUM

From western China, this spreads steadily by chains of little tubers, sending up small leaves with narrow divisions, deeply cut and toothed. The frail stems, up to 10in (25cm), are capped with trumpet-shaped rose-pink flowers 1in

(2.5cm), green centred and finely pencilled with darker veins in early summer. Conspicuous green sepals add to its charm. After flowering the plant becomes dormant until the following spring. Because of this brief appearance it is not a great threat to neighbouring plants in the rock garden – a sparse diet in full sun will help to restrain it and produce more flowers. It can be propagated by lifting and dividing the tubers, or by seed.

Geranium pyrenaicum

GERANIUM PYRENAICUM

Originally from south-western Europe. Be cautious about introducing this species to the small garden, for although the 12in (30cm) mounded rosettes of pleasantly aromatic, ever-green rounded leaves are decorative, the abundance of self-sown seedlings can be a real nuisance. They grow very quickly and can soon smother smaller plants. Rounded flowers ³⁄₄in (2cm), which are produced on thin, lax stems, are purplish-pink with notched petals, and continue blooming from late spring until autumn.

G.p. forma albiflorum has large white, starry flowers but is equally generous in its production of seedlings.

G.p. 'Bill Wallis' (often misspelt 'Bill Wallace') is an eye-catching variation with strong purple flowers, just as prolific as the type. It is named after the late Bill Wallis, who introduced it from his nursery in Cambridgeshire, the well-named Useful Plant Company!

G. 'Rebecca', see page 77 for a list of Alan Bremner's hybrids.

GERANIUM RECTUM

A native of central Asia, Chinese Turkestan and the north-western Himalayas. *G. rectum* is a clump-forming species with sharply toothed leaves similar to those of *G. endressii*, but the lobes are broader and shorter. The flowers 1in (2.5cm) are carried from early summer into autumn on loosely spreading stems and are bright rose-pink with a white centre and dark crimson veins. Although not a particularly garden-worthy plant, it could find a place in the woodland garden or in a shady corner under shrubs. It is propagated by division or seed.

GERANIUM REFLEXUM

From Italy, Yugoslavia and northern Greece, *G. reflexum* resembles *G. phaeum*, with boldly blotched leaves and flowers ³⁄₄in (2cm) which have narrower, strongly reflexed rose-pink petals, a white centre edged with a bluish band and reddish sepals. Pleasant ground cover for dry, shady places; propagated by division or seed.

GERANIUM REFRACTUM

Originally from the Himalayas, northern Burma and south-western China, this species has only recently been introduced to cultivation in the UK. It is 24in (60cm) and has a compact rootstock and deeply divided palmate leaves which are sometimes marbled. Its nodding flowers are white or pale pink (very occasionally reddish-purple) with narrow reflexed petals, blue-black anthers and purplish sepals. It has coarse, purple glandular hairs on its upper parts. Propagation is by seed or possibly by division.

GERANIUM RENARDII

From the Caucasus, *G. renardii* is a great favourite, highly valued as a foliage plant. It forms neat clumps 12in (30cm) high, of soft sage green, wrinkled leaves, velvety in texture, rounded and divided to about half-way. Flowers, produced from early summer to mid-summer, 1¼in (3cm) are opal white with pronounced purple veins, and wedge-shaped petals which are notched and widely spaced. Suitable for the rock garden or the front of a border, it is sometimes reluctant to flower, but a sparse diet in full sun will help to overcome this problem.

G.r. 'Whiteknights' is a lilac-blue flowered form, the name referring to the place of origin at Reading University, Berkshire. Both forms may be propagated by division.

Geranium renardii

GERANIUM RICHARDSONII

Western North America is the home of this variable species that grows in damp places in the wild, and is therefore not too happy in dry conditions in the garden. Good forms are very attractive and are between 12–24in (30–60cm) in height. The bright green, glossy leaves are deeply lobed. The flat flowers 1¼in (3cm) are usually white though occasionally pale pink,

sometimes veined with pale purplish-pink, with anthers of mauvish-grey. *G. richardsonii* is a lovely border plant where soil retains moisture, in the wild garden or at the streamside. It benefits from being replanted if the roots become exposed, and may be increased by division or seed.

Geranium × riversleaianum 'Russell Prichard'

GERANIUM × RIVERSLEAIANUM
(*G. endressii* × *G. traversii*)

Several cultivars have arisen from this cross. The two described here are widely available, both are sterile but are easily divided, preferably in spring.

G. × r. 'Mavis Simpson' is a seedling which occurred at Kew. It makes low, wide-spreading mats of small, silvery, silky, pale green leaves. Countless prettily rounded shell-pink flowers 1in (2.5cm) are overlaid with a silvery sheen and darker veins and are continuously produced on long trailing stems throughout summer and autumn, until cut back by frost. This is a delightful cranesbill for the rock garden, raised bed or front of the border in full sun. It looks lovely weaving through *Cosmos atrosanguineus*, with purple foliage such as *Heuchera micrantha* 'Palace Purple', *Salvia officinalis* 'Purpurascens', and the purple-leaved plantain (*Plantago major* 'Rubrifolia').

G. × r. 'Russell Prichard' is the original clonal cultivar, which was raised at Prichard's nursery at Riverslea in Hampshire, both now being commemorated in the name. It is similar to 'Mavis Simpson' but with flowers of bright magenta-pink. It is not quite so hardy and protection of the crown is advisable in winter. Old growth tends to die out from the middle, but regular division in spring helps to keep it in good condition.

GERANIUM RIVULARE
(syn G. *aconitifolium*, G. *sylvaticum* subsp. *rivulare*)

Originated in the western and central European Alps. It is an erect plant up to 18in (45cm) high, with leaves very deeply cut into narrow, long and sharply toothed divisions. Small but numerous flowers 3/8–1in (1–2.5cm) occur in early summer; these are funnel-shaped and white in colour with fine violet veins. This is a quietly charming geranium which is easily grown in sun or shade and any reasonable soil. It may be increased by division or seed.

GERANIUM ROBERTIANUM

A widespread geranium, described under British Natives. The Herb Robert is welcome in the wild garden, where it can seed with abandon. A compact cultivar, *G. robertianum* 'Celtic White' makes flat rosettes of light green, filigree leaves, above which tiny, pure white flowers appear for weeks on end. It is very endearing, though equally as free-seeding as the type, and can be troublesome if admitted to the rock garden.

GERANIUM RUBESCENS

A native of Madeira, *G. rubescens* is a biennial and is like a large Herb Robert 24–36in (61–91cm) high, with glossy beetroot-red stems and leaf stalks. The leaves, which are deeply cut, profusely lobed and toothed, turn brilliant red in autumn. The bright pink flowers 1in (2.5cm) have pale veins and a small crimson-red eye, and are produced from early summer to autumn. *G. rubescens* is the hardiest of all these giant rosette-forming geraniums, and will naturalise in a sheltered corner where the soil is not too heavy and wet, making an impressive winter feature. New plants are easily raised from seed.

GERANIUM RUBIFOLIUM

From Kashmir, the name of this species refers to *Rubus* (bramble) but the leaves also resemble those of *G. nodosum*, with a wrinkled surface. Growing from a sturdy root system, *G. rubifolium* sends up masses of thin branching stems 40–70in (102–178cm) topped with ample, rounded flowers 1–1¼in (2.5–3cm) of a purplish-violet colour, finely veined and white at the centre. They carry on blooming all summer and often later. Although quite hardy, *G. rubifolium* dislikes wet feet especially in winter, when it is apt to disappear without trace. A situation in the angle of two walls on light, well-drained soil in partial shade would be ideal for this charming species. Seed germinates very freely, but the young plants need care, and protection from damp. Division may be possible, but has not yet been tried personally.

GERANIUM RUPRETCHII

A little-known species from Russia and the Caucasus, *G. rupretchii* is similar to *G. pratense* though with larger, fewer dark violet flowers.

GERANIUM 'SALOME'
(G. *lambertii* × G. *procurrens*)

Introduced by Elizabeth Strangman of Washfield Nursery in Kent, from a seedling that appeared in her garden. Like *G. lambertii* in habit, 'Salome' forms a mound of faintly marbled leaves, gold-tinged when young. Sultry flowers 1¼in (3cm) of an unusual dusky violet-pink are heavily veined with darker violet and a dark central zone. It has a long flowering season from mid-summer to late autumn and can be propagated from stem cuttings.

GERANIUM SANGUINEUM

From Europe, the Caucasus and northern Turkey, this species is also known as the Bloody Cranesbill. It forms low mats 9–12in (23–30cm) of tangled, leafy stems. The small, rounded leaves are very deeply divided into narrow segments which are cut again into three sharply toothed lobes. In autumn they assume intriguing tints of orange, rusty-brown, brilliant red and finally dark brown. The typical plant has purple-magenta saucer-shaped flowers 1–1½in (2.5–3cm) from early summer to autumn. It is an ideal plant for the cottage garden, but is also at home in the rock garden, paving, raised bed or trailing over walls, in sun or part shade. It is easily divided for propagation, though seed may be variable. There are a number of good garden cultivars.

G.s. 'Alan Bloom' is a new introduction from Bloom's Nursery – named after the founder in honour of his eighty-fifth birthday. It has masses of large, bright pink flowers which cover the luxuriant foliage for weeks from early summer.

G.s. 'Album' is a looser, taller plant with lovely white flowers on rather straggling stems.

G.s. 'Cedric Morris' is a particularly large-flowered, magenta-pink form with larger leaves, discovered by Cedric Morris on the Gower Coast in Wales.

G.s. 'Elsbeth' is a recent introduction with large flowers of bright purple.

G.s. 'Glenluce' was discovered by A.T. Johnson in 1937 near Glenluce in Scotland. It has large flowers in a distinctive shade of rose-pink.

G.s. 'Holden' syn. 'Holden's Variety' and 'Holden's Form' was raised by Dr Milne-Redhead at Holden Clough Nursery in Lancashire. It was described in their 1972 catalogue as, 'Holden's Form – a pure pink form of our native plant, semi-prostrate, 6in' (15cm).

Geranium sanguineum

G.s. 'Jubilee Pink' was raised by Jack Drake at Inshriach Nursery, Aviemore, Scotland c1975. It has mounds of dark green foliage 10in (25cm) high, covered all summer in quantities of large 1½in (4cm) bright magenta-pink flowers with notched petals. It was awarded a First Class Certificate in 1976 after the Wisley Trials.

G.s. 'Max Frei' a recent introduction from Germany, forms neat, rounded hummocks 8in (20cm) high and masses of deep magenta flowers, followed by good autumn leaf colour.

G.s. 'Minutum' is a very compact, prostrate plant with small leaves. Other dwarf forms such as G.s. 'Nanum' and G.s. 'Prostratum' sometimes appear in catalogues, but the validity of these names is doubtful.

G.s. 'Shepherd's Warning' was raised by Jack Drake and is very similar to G.s. 'Jubilee Pink', though the flowers are slightly smaller and deeper in colour. At the Wisley Trials it was rated lower than G.s. 'Jubilee Pink', only receiving a Highly Commended award, but has since proved to be a better and more compact plant.

G.s. var. striatum (syn. G.s. lancastriense) was discovered on Walney Island in Lancashire (now part of Cumbria). It is variable in the wild but the one grown in gardens is generally considered to be the loveliest of all the many forms of G. sanguineum. Its large flowers of the palest blush-pink, delicately veined with deeper pink, are produced over a very long season.

The white form of G. *sanguineum* is more refined than the type, with pure white flowers held well above the leaves on thin stems

A particularly large-flowered form of G. *sanguineum* was discovered on the Gower Peninsula in Wales by the artist and plantsman Cedric Morris, after whom it is named

G. 'Sea Fire', 'Sea Pink' and **'Sea Spray',** see page 77 for a list of Alan Bremner's hybrids.

GERANIUM SCHIEDEANUM
(syn. *G. purpusii*)

Originally from Mexico, this is a low, sprawling plant arising from a thick rootstock. It has much divided, roundish or kidney-shaped leaves, a slightly glossy, wrinkled surface with a greyish and hairy underside. The flowers, produced all summer, are 1¼in (3cm) across, held on thin, reddish stems and are lilac with pink veins and notched petals. Though not reliably hardy, it may survive outside in warmer areas, in well-drained soil in the rock garden or front of the border. It is easily divided for propagation or raised from seed, but this is not very freely produced.

GERANIUM SESSILIFLORUM
subsp. *NOVAEZELANDIAE*

A subspecies from New Zealand that forms neat rosettes of small rounded green leaves, in which little white flowers ⅜in (1cm) nestle all through the summer.

G.s. subsp. *n.* 'Nigricans' is the form most often grown on account of its fascinating bronze foliage, which varies considerably in colour from pale to dark brown, enlivened by the occasional orange leaf. There are also some good, dark red leaved forms. All are best against a light background such as shingle or paving. There are always plenty of self-sown seedlings.

GERANIUM SHIKOKIANUM

Originally from southern Japan and Korea, this is a bushy plant up to 16in (40cm) with deeply cut, nicely marbled leaves, most of which are borne on the long thin flowering stalks. The funnel-shaped flowers 1in (2.5cm) are rose-pink with purple netted veins, a white centre and blue anthers. This attractive geranium dislikes being dried out, and prefers light shade. Flower-ing from mid-summer into autumn, it adds in-terest to low shrubs with dull foliage by weaving through the branches. It is easily divided or raised from seed.

GERANIUM SIBIRICUM

A sprawling species from eastern and central Europe, CIS, China, Japan and the Himalayas, with light green, deeply cut, narrowly lobed and sharply toothed leaves. Small flowers ⅜in (1cm) across, are white or pale pink with dark veins. It has no real garden value.

GERANIUM SINENSE

A native of south-western China, *G. sinense* was formerly known incorrectly as *G. delavayi*, which is probably not in cultivation. *G. sinense* is a very distinguished, fascinating species, grow-ing up to 24in (61cm) in height. It forms a mound of dark, shiny, faintly marbled leaves which are deeply divided into seven lobes. Its in-verted flowers ¾in (2cm) are similar in shape to those of *G. phaeum*. They are a gorgeous dark maroon, almost black, with velvety reflexed petals, coral-pink at the base. A distinctive red beak tipped with bluish-black anthers adds to the individuality of this elegant cranesbill, which starts to bloom in late summer. A partly shaded border or woodland garden will suit it, though it will also grow in full sun if not too dry. Siting it on a raised bed or bank will enable you to appreciate its upside-down detail without too great a contortion. It can be propagated by divi-sion or seed, though seedlings take two or three years to reach the flowering stage.

GERANIUM SOBOLIFERUM

A native of CIS, Manchuria, and the mountains of central and southern Japan, this is a small, compact geranium 12–15in (30–38cm) high, with finely cut ferny leaves. The saucer-shaped flowers 1¼in (3cm) are purplish-red with dark veins and are produced over a long period from mid-summer into autumn. *G. soboliferum* is rather difficult to please, needing very moist soil, preferably in sun. It was one of the few geranium casualties in my garden during a recent drought-ridden summer. Planting it at the stream side or the edge of a pond might be the answer. Propagation is by division or seed.

GERANIUM 'SPINNERS'
(*G. pratense* × ?)

Introduced by Axletree Nursery in 1990. It was raised by Peter Chappell of Spinners Nursery in Hampshire in the mid-1980s from seed originating in western North America, supplied by the late Marvin Black. It was originally distributed under the name *G. bergianum* or sometimes as G. 'Kashmir Purple'. The exact parentage is not known, but G. 'Spinners' is a splendid plant, making large clumps of deeply divided leaves. Tall stems up to 36in (91cm) are topped with a wealth of deep purplish-blue, bowl-shaped flowers, 1¼in (3cm) across from late spring to mid-summer. It is lovely growing through *Artemisia* 'Lambrook Silver' which will support its stems. Propagation is by division.

G. 'Spinners' has an upright habit and strong growth derived from *G. pratense*; the other parent of this hybrid is unknown. Originally grown from seed sent from USA by the late Marvin Black, it was raised by Peter Chappell at his Hampshire nursery, from where it gets its name

GERANIUM 'STANHOE'
(G. sessiliflorum × G. traversii)

Frequently misspelt 'Standhoe', this hybrid occurred in the garden of Ken and Gillian Beckett at Stanhoe near King's Lynn in Norfolk. It is similar in habit to G. *traversii*, though the leaves are greener and slightly smaller, with the divisions overlapping. Delicate pink flowers ¾in (2cm) with translucent veins on trailing stems, are produced from mid-summer to autumn. It makes a good trough or rock garden plant, in full sun and gritty soil. Propagation is easy from division or stem cuttings, but the seed will be very variable.

GERANIUM STAPFIANUM

A dwarf species from south-western China and south-eastern Tibet. It stands 6in (15cm) high, spreading by underground stolons, and has smallish, kidney-shaped, deeply cut, marbled leaves. The attractive, large flowers 1½in (4cm) are a deep reddish-magenta, with dark well-defined veins, a reddish centre and notched petals. The leaf and flower stems, the sepals, style and stigmas are all red. Growing on rocks and cliffs in the wild, it adapts to the scree bed where the conditions are not too hot and dry, or could be tried in the alpine house. This is not the plant which in the past was mistakenly sold as G. *stapfianum roseum*, which has now been identified by Dr Yeo as G. *orientalitibeticum*.

GERANIUM SUBULATO-STIPULATUM

The name of this species from North America and Mexico has such a nice rhythm, it should be worth growing for that alone! Seed of this species is sometimes listed by specialist societies. It has deeply divided, sharply toothed leaves, magenta to dark lilac flowers ½in (1.5cm) across with a few darker veins, and long trailing stems which reach up to 31in (80cm). My seedlings have not yet flowered so at the moment I am unable to comment on hardiness or garden value.

GERANIUM SWATENSE

From the Swat region of Pakistan, this is a low, sprawling hairy plant growing from a thick taproot, with few or no basal leaves. Its deeply cut, marbled kidney-shaped leaves are borne in pairs on thin, reddish trailing stems up to 20in (50cm). Large flattish flowers 1½in (4cm) are bright purplish-pink with a small white eye and purplish anthers; green sepals change to purplish-brown as the flowers develop in summer. It is not long-lived in my garden, probably needing a more open, sunny position in the rock garden or scree bed. Propagation is by seed, which germinates freely.

GERANIUM SYLVATICUM

A native of Europe and northern Turkey. The wood cranesbill and its various forms are useful garden plants, flowering in late spring, before the majority of other hardy geraniums. Inhabiting damp meadows in the wild, they will grow well in ordinary garden soil, though they really give their best in places which are not too dry. Reaching 28in (70cm) they make compact clumps of deeply, rather broadly divided leaves which are prettily lobed and toothed. Saucer-shaped flowers ¾–1¼in (2–3cm) vary in the wild from white and pink to pinkish-purple, with a white centre. A number of good garden forms are available. All can be divided but seed will be variable.

G.s. forma *albiflorum* (not to be confused with G. *albiflorum*, which is shorter) is the name given to the white-flowered variants in the wild. **G.s.** album is a beautiful cultivar with large, pure white flowers and good foliage – ideal for the 'white' garden. It comes true from seed. **G.s.** 'Amy Doncaster' is named after the discerning plantswoman who selected the plant for its striking deep blue, white-eyed flowers and excellent foliage. This is the bluest of all the G. *sylvaticum* forms. **G.s.** 'Baker's Pink', (originally known as G. 'Wengen') is a lovely, soft, clear pink form with

G. *sylvaticum* 'Mayflower' has richly coloured flowers in spring, and benefits from being cut-back after the main flush; this encourages new growth for later effect

large flowers that was discovered in the Swiss Alps by A.W.A. ('Bill') Baker. It is a robust, tall plant, flowering a little later than the type, but very floriferous over a long period.

G.s. 'Mayflower' was introduced by Bloom's Nurseries. A particularly attractive clone, it has large, rich violet-blue flowers with a white eye and is a good companion for *Dicentra spectabilis alba* and white-flowered variegated honesty.

G.s. forma *roseum* is a pink-flowered variant.

G.s. var. *wanneri* has plum-pink flowers with bright pink veins.

GERANIUM THUNBERGII

A vigorous, sprawling cranesbill with its origins in northern China, Taiwan and Japan. It has light green, semi-evergreen foliage and is 9in (23cm) in height. The leaves are deeply cut into broad lobes with dark marks in the notches. Trailing stems bear small flowers 1/2–3/4in (1.5–2cm)

from late summer into autumn, varying from white to rose-purple with purple veins. G. *thunbergii* is a rather weedy species but makes quite useful ground cover for dry places. It can be propagated by seed or from the occasionally rooting stems.

GERANIUM TRANSBAICALICUM

Originally from Siberia, this is a regional variant of G. *pratense*. Seed received from Moscow Botanic Garden some years ago resulted in compact plants 10in (25cm) high, with deeply and finely divided feathery leaves, the flowers similar to those of G. *pratense*, but a rather deep mauve-blue. Since then, seed from another source has produced much taller plants 24–30in (61–76cm) with weak, flopping stems, flowering prolifically over a very long season. It looks delightful growing through *Rosa alba* 'Maiden's Blush'. Propagation is by division or seed.

GERANIUM TRAVERSII var. ELEGANS

This exquisite small plant was discovered by H.H. Travers on the coastal cliffs of the Chatham Islands, east of New Zealand. It makes compact mounds 6–8in (15–20cm) of small, rounded, softly hairy, grey-green leaves. Perfectly formed saucer-shaped flowers 1in (2.5cm) are a milky shell-pink, edged with paler pink, and are carried on their collapsing stems all through the summer months. Unfortunately it is not quite hardy, but grown in gritty soil on the rock garden, scree or trough – and given winter protection – it may survive quite happily. Propagate by cuttings or seed. A few self-sown seedlings quite often present themselves.

GERANIUM TRILOPHUM

An annual, originally from Africa, Asia and Iran. It is a rather slight species with small, deeply cut leaves and tiny flowers 3/8in (1cm), which are deep pink with dark veins converging at the centre. The flowers often refuse to open, but the fruits are intriguingly ridged and winged.

140

GERANIUM TUBEROSUM

A native of the Mediterranean region and east-wards to western Iran. As one would expect, a tuberous-rooted species, sending up very finely cut, feathery leaves in spring, then becoming dormant after flowering. The slender, erect stems 8–10in (20–25cm) high are topped by rosy-purple flowers 1in (2.5cm) with deeply notched petals, opening in early summer. The tubers spread rapidly, but it is reputed that the Chinese use them in cooking so you can always try eating the surplus!

GERANIUM VERSICOLOR
(syn. *G. striatum*)

Grown in gardens for over three hundred years, *G. versicolor* develops bushy clumps of light green leaves similar to those of *G. endressii* but with broader lobes and more rounded teeth. The leaves are usually brown-blotched between the divisions. Trumpet-shaped flowers 1in (2.5cm) are white with a close network of magenta veins and occur from early summer to autumn. Seeding abundantly and hybridising freely with *G. endressii*, *G. versicolor* provides useful naturalising ground cover which is easily increased by division.

GERANIUM VISCOSISSIMUM

A native of western North America, this is a sticky-haired plant resembling *G. nervosum* – the basal leaves being somewhat larger and less sharply toothed. Both species are variable and the differences are not always easily distinguished. The large flattish flowers 1¼–1½in (3–4cm) of *G. viscosissimum* vary from pale to purplish-pink, are darkly veined and usually have a white centre. A lovely plant, it carries its freely produced flowers in open clusters on tall branching stems up to 30in (76cm) in summer and often again in autumn. The deep, woody roots are not easy to divide, but seed germinates well. Originating in woods and meadows, it will adapt to sun or partial shade in gardens.

GERANIUM WALLICHIANUM

A Himalayan plant of low sprawling habit 12in (30cm) in height with a spread of about 36in (91cm). The shallowly divided, marbled leaves are held in pairs on diffuse stems. The flowers are saucer-shaped, 1–1⅜in (2.5–3.5cm), pinkish- or purplish-blue with a white centre and black stamens from late summer to late autumn. It is said to need a cool, moist root-run, but it performed exceptionally well in recent dry summers. *G. wallichianum* is ideal for trailing over low walls or weaving through neighbouring plants in the border. The stout taproot is not easy to divide, so seed is the best method of propagation.

Geranium wallichianum 'Buxton's Variety'

G.w. 'Buxton's Variety' syn. G.w. 'Buxton's Blue'. Although the typical plant is not to be despised, the form raised by E.C. Buxton in North Wales c.1920 is the one generally grown in gardens. The flowers are very appealing, a clear sky-blue with a large white centrepiece, enhanced by the black stamens. Seed comes nearly true, but selection of the seedlings with the clearest blue flowers is advisable.

G.w. 'Syabru'. Introduced from Nepal by Edward Needham, and named after the Sherpa village near which it was found. It is a strong grower, producing a mound of dark, rich green leaves and gorgeous bright magenta flowers over a long period.

GERANIUM WLASSOVIANUM

Originally from eastern Siberia, Mongolia and north-eastern China, G. *wlassovianum* is a clump-forming, hairy plant with attractive foliage, emerging pinkish-bronze in spring. The mature leaves are velvety in texture, dusky green tinged with brown, and assume brilliant red autumn colour, which darkens to purplish-brown before the leaves collapse. The flowers 1¼in (3cm) across, are a dusky purplish-violet with a small white eye and veined with deep violet. Growing in damp grassland and scrub in the wild, G. *wlassovianum* prefers soil that retains moisture. In cultivation it is suitable for the wild garden or front of the border, in sun or part shade. It is easily divided or raised from seed. In addition, it is recommended by Melvyn Crann in his booklet on hardy geraniums as being 'A satisfying name to speak through clenched teeth in time of stress'! Despite having so many points in its favour, G. *wlassovianum* is still not as well known as it should be.

GERANIUM YESOENSE

A native of central and northern Japan and the Kuril Islands to the north of Japan. This bushy cranesbill 12–16in (30–40cm) in height, has leaves which are deeply cut into sharply pointed divisions like those of G. *sanguineum*. The flowers, borne in summer, are saucer-shaped, pink with finely drawn darker veins, or occasionally white-petalled with no veining. Needing a moisture-retentive soil, G. *yesoense* is suitable for the wild garden, streamside or water garden and can be propagated by division or seed.

GERANIUM YUNNANENSE
(syn. G. *candicans*)

A recent introduction from south-western China (Yunnan) and northern Burma, G. *yunnanense* grows from a thick, compact root system, with marbled, broadly lobed and toothed leaves. Its nodding, bowl-shaped flowers 1¼–1½in (3–4cm) across are pink with black anthers and are produced in summer. The synonym G. *candicans* refers to a rare white form, although this name has also been incorrectly applied to G. *lambertii*. G. *yunnanense* can be propagated by division or seed.

BRITISH NATIVES

Geraniums endemic to the United Kingdom are included here for the sake of completeness, but although they look delightful in natural surroundings, very few are suitable for cultivation. There are also several species which, although not native, have become naturalised in the wild – these are known as 'garden escapes' and include such familiar plants as *Geranium endressii*, G. *nodosum*, G. *phaeum* and G. *versicolor*. Improved garden forms of these species are now available commercially, and are detailed in the main A–Z list.

GERANIUM COLUMBINUM

The Long-stalked Cranesbill is an annual – a slender plant with basal leaves more solid than the leaves on the stem and which are finely cut into narrow segments. The funnel-shaped flowers, borne in mid-summer, are pale or reddish-pink with a white eye and darker veins. The petals are sometimes notched. Inhabiting dry pastures, hedgerows and scrub, the Long-stalked Cranesbill is not without a certain charm and might be worth a place in the wild garden.

142

GERANIUM DISSECTUM

The Cut-leaved Cranesbill is a low-growing annual, a sprawling plant with stem-leaves deeply divided into narrow segments. It has small flowers, ⅜in (1cm), purplish-pink with deeply notched petals, that are produced all summer. It has a quiet charm in its natural habitat of hedgerows and waste places.

GERANIUM LUCIDUM

The Shining Cranesbill is also an annual. In spite of this cranesbill's prolific seeding habits, its low-key attractions are hard to resist. The rosettes of smooth, glossy green leaves form mounds up to 12in (30cm) (less in poor soil), with each leaf prettily rounded and divided into five. The leaf and flower stems are red in older plants, the leaves also reddening with age. There are small, dainty flowers ⅜in (1cm), produced over a long period, being deep pink with rounded petals. Found on shady rocks, walls and waste places, G. *lucidum* makes useful ground cover in garden areas where nothing much else will survive. In one of my gardens it colonised a very high sand bank and was most welcome.

GERANIUM MOLLE

Also known as the Dove's-foot Cranesbill, G. *molle* is an annual. Its leaves are round in shape, grey-green and softly hairy, forming attractive rosettes in early spring. Small flowers ⅜in (1cm) are pale or purplish-pink with deeply notched petals and bluish anthers, and are borne on semi-prostrate, softly hairy stems. G. *molle* has a long flowering season – from late spring to autumn – and is very common on both waste and cultivated land, but is only really suitable for the wildest garden.

GERANIUM PRATENSE

Also called Meadow Cranesbill. In the UK this perennial is mainly found growing wild in the southern half of England, where it makes a great

The double blue variety of the Meadow Cranesbill, G. *pratense* 'Plenum Caeruleum' has a charming display of loosely petalled flowers in a soft, old-fashioned blue, bringing an air of instant tradition to the garden

impact with its spectacular flowers in summer. It often colonises roadside verges. It is a strong, upright plant bearing much-branched stems 24–36in (61–91cm) though often taller, with large leaves divided into seven or nine lobes, each handsomely cut again into sharply pointed segments. Blue flowers always have a special appeal, those of the Meadow Cranesbill being no exception. Large, 1½in (4cm), and saucer-shaped, they are usually violet-blue, enhanced by delicate pinkish veins and dark anthers, but the colour is variable. Prolifically produced over a long period, they often have a second flush in autumn, especially if cut to the ground after the main flowering. For good garden varieties, see the A–Z list.

GERANIUM PURPUREUM

This annual is known as Lesser Herb Robert and Little Robin. It is a smaller-flowered form of G. *robertianum*, sometimes treated as a sub-species; it has narrower leaf segments and yellow stamens, and the foliage is said to be without the characteristic scent. Frequenting cliffs and rocky places in coastal areas, it is also sometimes found inland. It flowers all summer, tolerating more sun than *G. robertianum*, but is really only suitable for the wild garden or open woodland.

GERANIUM PUSILLUM

The Small-flowered Cranesbill is aptly named! It is an annual rather similar to *G. molle*, but its leaves are more narrowly cut, with a crimson spot marking each notch. Minute flowers ¼in (0.5cm) or less, are lilac with notched petals and bluish anthers. Found in cultivated fields, hedgerows and waste places, *G. pusillum* prefers light sandy soil. It is best not introduced into the garden, but will probably appear uninvited.

GERANIUM PYRENAICUM

A perennial with several common names – Pyrenean Cranesbill, Hedgerow Cranesbill, Mountain Cranesbill. It forms attractive mounds of nicely rounded, evergreen leaves, cut to about halfway. Its dainty, starry flowers ⅜–¾in (1–2cm) are borne in pairs on thin, trailing stems about 24in (61cm) long. These flowers are mauvish-pink or purplish with deeply notched petals and continue all summer and into autumn.

G.p. forma albiflorum is a good white form which has slightly larger flowers.

Both are very enthusiastic seeders. In spite of the name, it grows in fields, open woods and waste places, mainly in the south and east of England. Although pleasing enough to cultivate in less tidy gardens, it can become a nuisance.

GERANIUM ROBERTIANUM

Also known as Herb Robert or musk-scented geranium, this is an annual growing from succulent rosettes. This beguiling cranesbill has daintily cut ferny foliage, often red-tinted, on brown or reddish stems. The strong scent of the leaves has been variously described as delightful or obnoxious. Roy Genders in *The Scented Flora of the*

World (1977) wrote, 'Though so charming it gives off a peculiar odour, particularly pronounced after rain, when the smell is foxy'. Yet Eleanour Sinclair Rohde, who wrote a number of books about herbs, considered it to be 'the most sweetly scented of all wild geraniums'. Herb Robert produces flowers continually, even during mild spells in winter. They are small ⅜–¾in (1–2cm), bright pink or white with orange or red anthers and rounded petals. It often appears in the garden uninvited, looking delightful in the chink of a shady wall or paving. Turn your back, and it will soon cover the whole garden, bedding itself comfortably in your most treasured small plants – you have been warned!

GERANIUM ROTUNDIFOLIUM

The Round-leaved Cranesbill is an annual. As one would expect, it has rounded leaves, divided to about halfway, wavy-edged with a small crimson spot marking each notch. It has small, pink flowers with a white centre and bluish anthers, and wedge-shaped petals only slightly notched, which appear in mid-summer. It grows on cliffs, walls and banks, mainly in south and east England, but has no real garden value.

GERANIUM SANGUINEUM

The Bloody Cranesbill or, more politely, Blood-red Cranesbill, is a perennial, a low-growing, bushy plant found on dry rocks, sea cliffs and dunes, usually in limestone areas. Its flowers are purple-crimson or pink. See A – Z list for full description and good garden varieties.

GERANIUM SYLVATICUM

Known as Wood Cranesbill, this is a medium-sized, upright perennial with elegant, fingered leaves. The flowers, which occur in early summer, vary in colour, ranging from violet-blue, purplish-pink and pink to white. It is found in damp meadows and on roadside verges, mainly in northern England and Scotland. See A–Z list for full description and named forms.

G. 'Brookside'

G. *himalayense*

G. 'Spinners'

G. *himalayense* 'Irish Blue'

G. 'Nimbus'

G. 'Patricia'

G. 'Ann Folkard'

G. 'Philippe Vapelle'

SOUTH AFRICAN SPECIES

In recent years a number of South African species of geranium have been introduced to the UK. Some have proved reasonably hardy and are well worth trying for their beautiful foliage and abundance of flowers. Although most species mentioned below inhabit damp, rocky places and streamsides at high altitudes in the wild, they seem to do better in drier situations in gardens in the UK.

GERANIUM BRYCEI

From Lesotho and the Drakensberg Mountains, this is a perennial sub-shrub up to 40in (1m) but usually less in cultivation. It eventually develops several woody stems and substantial mounds of silvery, palmate leaves which have raised, brownish veins on the undersides. Their upper surface is clothed with shaggy, white hairs and they have densely matted white hairs below. Flowers up to 1½in (4cm) are borne on branched stems in mid-summer, varying in colour from pink, pale or deep violet to light magenta, sometimes with a white central eye. The petals are shallowly notched. *G. brycei* has not proved hardy in my garden in Somerset but might well survive in a sunny, sheltered position such as in the angle of a wall, on light soil. Propagation is by seed or cuttings.

GERANIUM CAFFRUM

From Kimberley, Albany and Zwartkops, this is a perennial, sprawling plant, 24in (61cm) growing from a long, thick taproot. Slender stems, woody at the base, root where they touch the soil. The leaves are very deeply cut into narrow lobes, each sharply toothed. In the wild the flowers are usually white or pale pink, but those in cultivation in the UK tend to be bright pink, 1in (2.5cm), giving a good display in summer. It seems to be reasonably hardy, if grown on a sunny well drained bank, but has not yet been tested by a severe winter in my garden. Seed

germinates readily, and rooted pieces can be detached as a means of propagation.

GERANIUM INCANUM
var. *MULTIFIDUM*

From the Cape – from Hout Bay to Port Alfred. This variety is the one generally grown in UK gardens – a bushy little plant somewhat trailing in habit, 8–9in (20–23cm) in height. It forms a delightful creation of light and airy filigree leaves, green above, silver beneath, often displaying deep red autumn tints. Crushed leaves have an aroma which is difficult to pinpoint, but vaguely reminiscent of parsley. Flowers are freely produced all summer 1–1½in (2.5–4cm), and are deep reddish-purple with darker veins and white centres, with narrowly notched petals. Though not reliably hardy, it may survive outside in mild winters, given gritty soil and a sunny sheltered position, cascading over the side of a trough or low wall or rambling over rocks. As a wise precaution, take cuttings in mid-summer. These will root quickly and make good plants by the spring, provided they can be given winter protection. Seed germinates freely, and self-sown seedlings sometimes appear.

GERANIUM PULCHRUM

A perennial from the Drakensberg range. It is a strong-growing, woody sub-shrub up to 40in (1m) but usually less, and is deservedly named 'pulchrum' which means beautiful. The leaves which are grey-green, have a soft, velvety texture – irresistible to touch. They have five to seven lobes, which are handsomely finger-shaped and sharply toothed. The upper surface is covered with silvery, silky hairs, which are denser on the underside. The flowers 1½in (4cm) are produced on much-branched stems in mid- to late summer, varying from mauvish-pink to deep pink, sometimes lighter or white at the centre, with shallowly notched petals. In my experience it has survived −10°C outside; in fact the plants over-wintering under cover are the ones that usually give up the ghost! It is best grown in sun or light shade in the border, in a large container or, most effectively, on a low bank with perhaps G. *asphodeloides* at its feet. Take cuttings fairly early in summer so that they can establish by winter. The germination rate of seed is high, and seedlings grow on very quickly.

GERANIUM ROBUSTUM

A perennial found in Natal, Transvaal, Orange Free State, Lesotho and Transkei. This geranium is a woody sub-shrub growing up to 40in (1m) with a wide spread of lovely, ferny, silvery grey-green leaves, more silvery on the underside. For sheer flower-power it is hard to beat. Borne in pairs, each flower is 1¼–1½in (3–4cm), pink or pale purple, and covering the whole bush all through summer. After all that effort it may look a bit bedraggled and can be cut back fairly hard. In no time the foliage will be replenished, and another crop of flowers produced. G. *robustum* makes an unusual border plant, mingling well with such companions as *Berberis* 'Rose Glow', *Heuchera* 'Palace Purple' and pink-flowered colchicums. From personal experience this seems to be the hardiest of the South African species so far grown, having survived outside in my garden for over ten years, first in Surrey and now in Somerset.

APPENDIX

WHERE TO SEE GERANIUMS

Here is a representative selection of gardens in which groups or collections of geraniums can be seen growing. Most of them are open to the public on behalf of the National Gardens Scheme Charitable Trust, and details of their opening times can be found in *Gardens of England and Wales* (known as 'The Yellow Book'), and *Scotland's Gardens Scheme*. Another annual publication which lists gardens in Great Britain and Ireland is *The Good Gardens Guide*, published by Vermilion and edited by Graham Rose and Peter King.

Some gardens also open by appointment, with prior arrangement, or for local charities. Most will have plants for sale, several have their own nurseries, notably Barnsley House, Greatham Mill, Herterton House, the Savill Garden, and the Royal Horticultural Society's garden at Wisley.

Buckinghamshire
Spindrift, Jordans Village, near Beaconsfield (Mr and Mrs E. Desmond)

Berkshire
Old Rectory Cottage, Tidmarsh, Pangbourne (Mr and Mrs A.W.A. Baker)

Cambridgeshire
Cambridge University Botanic Garden, Bateman Street

Cornwall
Trehane, near Probus (David and Simon Trehane)

Derbyshire
210 Nottingham Road, Woodlinkin, Langley Mill (Mr and Mrs R. Brown)

Devon
The Bungalow, 9 Bouchers Hill, North Tawton, near Okehampton (Dr and Mrs M.C. Corfield)

Dorset
Broadlands, Hazelbury Bryan, near Sturminster Newton (Mr and Mrs M.J. Smith)

Snape Cottage, Chaffey Moor, Bourton (Mr and Mrs I. Whinfield)
Little Platt, Plush (Sir Robert Williams)

Gloucestershire
Barnsley House, Barnsley (Mrs Rosemary Verey)
Kiftsgate Court, Chipping Campden (Mr and Mrs A.H. Chambers)
Trevi Garden, Hartpury (Mr and Mrs G.D. Gough)

Hampshire
Brandy Mount House, Brandy Mount, Alresford (Mr and Mrs M. Baron)
Greatham Mill, Greatham, near Liss (Mrs E.N. Pumphrey)
White Windows, Longparish, near Andover (Mr and Mrs B. Sterndale-Bennett)

Kent
Nettlestead Place, Nettlestead, Maidstone (Mr and Mrs R. Tucker)
The Old Parsonage, Sutton Valence (Dr and Mrs R. Perks)
Sissinghurst Castle, Sissinghurst, near Cranbrook (The National Trust)

Hertfordshire
Hatfield House, Hatfield (The Marquess and Marchioness of Salisbury)

Leicestershire
Rose Cottage, Owston, near Oakham (Mr J.D. Buchanan)

London
29 Addison Avenue, London W11 (off Holland Park Avenue) (Mr and Mrs D.B. Nicholson)

Northumberland
Herterton House, Hartington, Cambo, Morpeth (Mr and Mrs F. Lawley)

Shropshire
Benthall Hall, Broseley (The National Trust)

148

Staffordshire
Oulton House, Oulton, near Stone (Mr and Mrs J.E. Bridger)

Suffolk
Helmingham Hall, Stowmarket (Lord Tollemache)

Surrey
Hookwood Farm House, West Horsley (Mrs E.W. Mason)
Rise Top Cottage, off Maybourne Rise, Mayford, Woking (Trevor Bath)
The Royal Horticultural Society's Garden, Wisley, Woking (The RHS)
The Savill Garden, Wick Lane, Englefield Green (Crown Estate Commissioners)

Sussex
Nymans, Handcross, near Haywards Heath, West Sussex (The National Trust)
Wakehurst Place, Ardingly, near Haywards Heath, West Sussex (The National Trust/The Royal Botanic Gardens, Kew)

Scotland
Bent, Laurencekirk, Kincardineshire, Grampian (Mr and Mrs J. Mackie)
Malleny House Gardens, Balerno, Midlothian (National Trust for Scotland)

Wales
The Glamorgans
11 Arno Road, Little Coldbrook, Barry (Mrs D. Palmer)
Gwynedd and Anglesey
Sychnant, Penmaenmawr (Chandler and A. Williamson)

United States of America
Gardenview Horticultural Park, 16711 Pearl Road, Strongsville, Ohio 44136
Wave Hill, 675 W 252 Street, Bronx, New York, 10471

WHERE TO BUY GERANIUMS

UNITED KINGDOM

The following are the main specialist suppliers:

Axletree Nursery (D.J. Hibberd) Starvecrow Lane, Peasmarsh, Rye, East Sussex TN 31 6XL (No Mail Order)
Catforth Gardens (Judith Bradshaw and Chris Moore) Roots Lane, Catforth, Preston, Lancs PR4 0JB National Collection Holders (No Mail Order)
Charter House Nursery (John Ross) 2, Nunwood, Dumfries, Dumfries and Galloway, Scotland DG2 0HX
Croftway Nursery (Graham Spencer) Yapton Road, Barnham, Bognor Regis, West Sussex PO22 0BH
Coombland Gardens (Mrs Rosemary Lee) Coombland, Coneyhurst, Billingshurst, West Sussex RH14 9DG National Collection Holder
Crûg Farm Plants (Mr B. Wynn-Jones) Griffith's Crossing, Nr Caernafon, Gwynedd LL55 1TU (No Mail Order)
The Margery Fish Plant Nursery (Mark Stainer) East Lambrook Manor, East Lambrook, South Petherton, Somerset TA13 5HL National Collection Holder

The Nursery Further Afield (Gerald Sinclair) Evenley Road, Mixbury, Nr Brackley, Northamptonshire NN13 5YR (No Mail Order)

Toad Hall Produce (S.V. North) Frogmore, Weston-under-Penyard, Herefordshire HR9 5TQ

Other nurseries with some less usual varieties

Birkheads Cottage Garden Nursery (Mrs Christine Liddle) Birkheads Lane, Near Sunniside, Newcastle upon Tyne, Tyne and Wear NE16 5EL (No Mail Order, no catalogue)
Blackthorn Nursery (A.R. and S.B. White) Kilmeston, Alresford, Hants SO24 0NL (No Mail Order)
Bregover Plants (Jennifer Bousfield) Hillbrooke, Middlewood, North Hill, Launceston, Cornwall PL15 7NN
Blooms of Bressingham (Ken March) Diss, Norfolk IP22 2AB
Bloomsbury (Susan Oakley) Upper Lodge Farm, Padworth Common, Reading, Berks RG7 4JD (No Mail Order)
Bridgmere Nurseries (John Ravenscroft) Bridgmere, Near Nantwich, Cheshire CW5 7QB (No Mail Order, no catalogue)
Cally Gardens (M.C. Wickenden) Gatehouse of Fleet, Castle Douglas, Scotland DG7 2DJ
Corsley Mill (B.E.P. Quest-Ritson) Highfield House, Shrewton, Salisbury, Wilts SP3 4BU (Mail Order in winter only)

Cranesbill Nursery (Mrs S.M. Bates) White Cottage, Stock Green, Near Redditch, Worcs B96 6SZ (Mail Order in autumn only)

Donington Plants (D.W. Salt) Donington House, Main Road, Wrangle, Boston, Lincs PE22 9AT

Eastgrove Cottage Garden Nursery (Malcolm and Carol Skinner) Sankyns Green, Near Shrawley, Little Witley, Worcs WR6 6LQ (No Mail Order)

Elworthy Cottage Garden Plants (Mrs J.M. Spiller) Elworthy Cottage, Elworthy, Lydeard St Lawrence, Taunton, Somerset TA4 3PX (No Mail Order)

Kaytie Fisher (Kaytie Fisher) The Nursery, South End Cottage, Long Reach, Ockham, Surrey GU23 6PF

Gannock Growers (Penny Pyle) Gannock Thatch, Sandon, Buntingford, Herts SG9 0RH

Garden Cottage Nursery (R. Rushbrooke) Tournaig, Poolewe, Achnasheen, Ross-shire IV22 2LH

Glebe Cottage Plants (Carol Klein) Pixie Lane, Warkleigh, Umberleigh, North Devon EX37 9DH (No Mail Order)

Henllys Lodge Plants (Mrs E. Lane) Henllys Lodge, Beaumaris, Anglesey, Gwynedd LL58 8HU

Holden Clough Nursery (P.J. Foley) Holden, Bolton-by-Bowland, Clitheroe, Lancs BB7 4PF

Hunts Court Garden and Nursery (T.K. and M.M. Marshall) North Nibley, Dursley, Glos GL11 6DZ (No Mail Order)

Kayes Garden Nursery (J.E. and Hazel Kaye) 1700 Melton Road, Rearsby, Leics LE7 8YR (No Mail Order)

Langthorns Plantery (P. and D. Cannon) High Cross Lane West, Little Canfield, Dunmow, Essex CM6 1TD (No Mail Order)

Mill Cottage Plants (Sally Gregson) The Mill, Henley Lane, Wookey, Nr Wells, Somerset BA5 1AP

Monksilver Nursery (Joe Sharman and Alan Leslie) Oakington Road, Cottenham, Cambridgeshire CB4 4TW

Orchard Nurseries (R. and J. Blenkinship) The Orchard, Tow Lane, Foston, Grantham, Lincs NG32 2LE

Rushfields of Ledbury (B. and J. Homewood) Ross Road, Ledbury, Herefordshire HR8 2LP

Spinners (Mark Fillan) Boldre, Lymington, Hampshire SO41 5QE (No Mail Order)

Stillingfleet Lodge Nurseries (Vanessa Cook) Stillingfleet, Yorks YO4 6HW

Sunbeam Nurseries (Noel Kingsbury) Bristol Road, Frampton Cotterell, Avon BS17 2AU

Tollgate Cottage Nursery (Brenda Timms) Ladbroke, Leamington Spa, Warwickshire CV33 0BY

Unusual Plants (Rosemary Shelley) Beth Chatto Gardens, Elmstead Market, Colchester, Essex CO7 7DB

Usual and Unusual Plants (Jennie Maillard) Onslow House, Magham Down, Hailsham, East Sussex BN27 1PL (No Mail Order)

Washfield Nursery (Elizabeth Strangman) Horns Road, Hawkhurst, Kent TN18 4QU (No Mail Order)

Most of these nurseries have display gardens, where geraniums and other plants can be seen growing. For full details, including opening times, please consult the current edition of *The Plant Finder*.

NORTH AMERICA

American Ornamental Perennials (Steve & Katsy Schmidt) P.O. Box 385, Gresham OR 97030

Canyon Creek Nursery (John Whittlesey) 3527 Dry Creek Road, Oroville CA 95965

Carroll Gardens P.O. Box 310, Westminster, MD 21157

Creative Garden Designs (Barbara Ashman) 8560 SW Fairway Drive, Portland OR 97225

Cricklewood Nursery (Don & Evie Douglas) 11907 Nevers Road, Snohomish WA 98290

Fancy Fronds (Judith Jones) 9111 4th Avenue West, Seattle WA 98119

Gardens by Design (Bob Ross) 1775 NW 113th Street, Portland OR 97229

Geraniaceae (Robin Parer) 122 Hillcrest Avenue, Kentfield CA 94904

Holbrook Farm and Nursery 115 Lance Road, P.O. Box 368, Fletcher NC 28732

Lamb Nurseries E101 Sharp Avenue, Spokane WA 99202

Log House Plants (Alice Doyle) 78185 Rat Creek Road, Cottage Grove OR 97424

Milaeger's Gardens 4838 Douglas Avenue, Racine WI 53402

The Primrose Path RD2 Box 110, Scottdale PA 15683

Rain Forest Gardens (Elke & Ken Knechtel) 13139 224th Street, RR 2, Maple Ridge BC V2X 7E7 Canada

Stonecrop Nurseries (Caroline Burgess) Box 371, RR 2, Coldspring NY 10516

Van Hevelingen Herb Nursery (Andrew & Melissa Van Hevelingen) 3113 N. Chehalem Drive, Newberg OR 97132

AUSTRALIA

Coffields Nursery (Rene Coffield) P.O. Box 102, Creswick, Victoria 3363

Digger's Garden Club (Clive Blazey) 105 La Trobe Parade, Dromana, Victoria 3936

Lambley Nursery (David Glenn) P.O. Box 142, Olinda, Victoria 3788

Norgates Flower Farm (Denis Norgate) Blackwood, Trentham Road, Victoria 3458

Rokewood Nursery (Felicity Kent) Sims Road, Mt Barker, South Australia 5251

Romantic Cottage Gardens (Graham Cooke) Bromany Brush, Boundary Road, Dromana, Victoria 3936

Viburnum Gardens (Michael Pitkin) 8 Sunnyridge Road, Arcadia, New South Wales 2159

Woodbank Nursery (Ken Gillanders) RMB 303, Kingston, Tasmania 7150

READING ABOUT GERANIUMS

Chivers, Susan and Woloszynska, Suzanne *The Cottage Garden: Margery Fish at East Lambrook Manor* (John Murray, 1990)

Fish, Margery *Gardening in the Shade* (Faber paperback, 1983)

Fish, Margery *Ground Cover Plants* (Faber paperback, 1980)

Fitter, R, Fitter A, and Blamey, Marjorie *The Wild Flowers of Britain and Northern Europe* (Collins paperback, 1974)

Taylor, Jane *Collecting Garden Plants* (Dent, 1989)

Thomas, Graham Stuart *Perennial Garden Plants* (Originally published Dent, 1976; now in 3rd edition, published in US by Sagapress/Timber Press)

Thomas, Graham Stuart *Plants for Ground Cover* (Dent paperback, 1990, published in US by Sagapress/Timber Press)

Verey, Rosemary *Good Planting* (Frances Lincoln, 1990)

Yeo, Peter F. *Hardy Geraniums* (Reprinted Batsford, 1992, published in US by Timber Press)

The following out-of-print books are well worth trying to obtain through libraries, or secondhand bookshops:

Beckett, Kenneth A. *Growing Hardy Perennials* (Croom Helm, 1981)

Bowles E.A. *My Garden in Summer* (Jack, 1914. Reprinted David & Charles 1974)

Johnson, A.T. *A Garden in Wales* (Edward Arnold, 1927)

Johnson, A.T. *A Woodland Garden* (Country Life, 1937)

Keble, Martin W. *The Concise British Flora in Colour* (Ebury Press and Michael Joseph, 1965)

SPECIALIST SOCIETIES

UNITED KINGDOM

The Hardy Plant Society Administrator: Mrs Pam Adams, Little Orchard, Great Comberton, Near Pershore, Worcestershire WR10 3DP

The British Pelargonium and Geranium Society Hon. Secretaries: Mr and Mrs R. Helyar, 134 Montrose Avenue, Welling, Kent, DA16 2QY

The Geraniaceae Group Membership Secretary: Ms Penny Clifton, 9 Waingate Bridge Cottages, Haverigg, Cumbria, LA18 4NF

THE AUTHORS

The writing of this book was allocated as follows: Joy Jones wrote the plant descriptions – the A-Z list, the British natives, the South African species and Alan Bremner's hybrids. Trevor Bath wrote the remainder except where individual contributors are given by-lines.

BILL BAKER has travelled widely in search of plants, several of which have been named after him. His delightfully eclectic garden in Berkshire has been given wide coverage in the gardening press and on television.

ROY LANCASTER F.I. Hort., FLS, VMM, VMH is a well-known and popular plantsman, lecturer, writer and broadcaster. His books include *Plant Hunting in Nepal*, *Travels in China* and *Garden Plants for Connoisseurs*. He also contributes regularly to *The Garden* magazine.

TREVOR NOTTLE is an Australian garden historian and lecturer. His books include *Cottage Garden Flowers*, *Growing Perennials* and the forthcoming *Gardens of the Sun*.

ALLAN ROBINSON is a member of the Robinson family who ran the fondly remembered hardy plant nursery at Swanley in Kent for many years. He is now in charge of the rock garden section at the Royal Horticultural Society's garden at Wisley in Surrey.

ROSEMARY VEREY is a distinguished writer, plantswoman, lecturer and authority on old herbals. Her fascinating garden at Barnsley House in Gloucestershire contains re-creations of many historical features, such as knot gardens and a potager, but it is also an outstanding example of good planting.

PETER F. YEO is a taxonomist based at the Cambridge Botanic Garden and a Fellow of the Linnean Society of London. His authoritative book *Hardy Geraniums*, published in 1985 and reprinted in 1992, has proved to be required reading and essential reference for everyone interested in the subject.

ACKNOWLEDGEMENTS

Special thanks to Melvyn Crann for permission to quote an extract from the Harlow Carr booklet on Geraniums, to the Hardy Plant Society for permission to include drawings by Peggy Dawe of G. × *monacense*, G. *pratense*, G. *renardii* and G. *sanguineum* which first appeared in the HPS booklet *'Hardy Geraniums for the Garden'*, and to John Bond, Alan Bloom, Alan Bremner, S. Millar Gault, Joan and Robin Grout, Andrew Norton, Faith Raven, Kay Sanecki, Graham Stuart Thomas and Peter F. Yeo for providing information and answering queries. Plant material for studio shots provided by Sarah Mason, Rosemary Lee (Coombland Gardens), Rita Baroux and Trevor Bath.

PHOTOGRAPHY
Studio shots Derek Croucher p. 9, 48, 51, 55, 60, 71, 98, 144.
John Fielding: p. 40, 94, 119; Andrew Lawson: p. 11, 42; John Glover: p. 2, 34; Clive Nichols: p. 21 (taken at Lower Severalls, Somerset); Harry Smith Collection: p. 17, 88; Trevor Bath p. 41. All other photographs are by Les Phillips.

Line drawings by Peggy Dawe.

INDEX

Page numbers in *italic* refer to illustrations

Aslet, Ken, 108
Associations
    Around the Shrubs, 26–9
    Bold Grouping, 14–19
    Double Delights, 22–4
    Dry Shady Places, 36–8
    Dry Sunny Places, 38–40
    Extending the Season,
        31–2
    A Family Group, 49
    Foliage Effect, 49, 50, 52
    Front Row, 30–1
    Gravel or Scree Beds, 44–6
    Moist Shady Corners,
        40–4
    Pale Surprise, 19–22
    Rough Grass, 47, 49
    Sinks and Containers,
        46–7
    A Touch of the Blues,
        24–5
    Trailing Geraniums,
        29–30
    Underplanting Roses,
        32–5
Axletree Nursery, 26, 76,
    77, 105, 106, 111, 122,
    123

Baker, Bill, 66, 70–3, 138–9
Beckett, Ken and Gillian,
    138
Black, Marvin, 86, 137
Blackthorn Nursery, 109
Bloody Cranesbill *see*
    G. sanguineum
Bloom, Alan, 66
Bloom's Nurseries 25, 45,
    108, 116, 130, 139
Bowles, E.A. 38, 64
Bradshaw, Judith, 83
Bremner, Alan, 73–7
Buxton, E.C., 64, 140

Cally Gardens, 77
Cambridge Botanic Garden,
    78, 107
Cantwell, Elaine Baxter, 87
Catforth Gardens, 83–4
Chappell, Peter, 137
Charterhouse Nursery, 77
Cherry Hinton Hall, 79

Claridge Druce, Dr, 37
Coats, Alice, 24
Coombland Gardens, 82
Crann, Melvyn, 49–50, 141
Cultivation, 53, 54, 56
Cut-leaved Cranesbill
    see G. dissectum

Douglas, Dan and Evie, 86,
    88–9
Dove's Foot Cranesbill *see*
    G. molle
Drake, Jack, 134

East Lambrook Manor
    Gardens, 85

Farrer, Reginald, 47, 111
Fish, Margery, 10, 12, 19,
    66, 85, 124
Fox, Robin Lane, 36

Gault, S.M., 25, 36
Genders, Roy, 143
Geranium
    *aconitifolium see G.
        rivulare*
    'Alanah' *see G. ×
        lindavicum* 'Alanah'
    'Alan Bloom' *see G.
        sanguineum* 'Alan
        Bloom'
    albanum, 34, 52, 102
    albiflorum, 102
    'Amy Doncaster' *see G.
        sylvaticum* 'Amy
        Doncaster'
    *anemonifolium see G.
        palmatum*
    'Ann Folkard', 29–30, 48,
        102, *103*, *144*
    'Anne Thompson', 75
    'Apple Blossom' *see G. ×
        lindavicum* 'Apple
        Blossom'
    argenteum, 46, 103
    aristatum, 31, 104, *104*
    *armenum see G.
        psilostemon*
    asphodeloides, 25, 30, 31,
        33, *58*, 104, *104*, *106*
        ssp. *asphodeloides*, 105

ssp. *crenophilum*, 105
ssp. *sintenisii*, 105
    'Prince Regent', 105
    'Starlight', 22, 105
'A.T. Johnson, *see G. ×
    oxonianum* 'A.T.
    Johnson'
*atlanticum see G.
    malviflorum*
'Baker's Pink' *see G.
    sylvaticum* 'Baker's
    Pink'
'Ballerina' *see G. cinereum*
    'Ballerina'
bergianum see G. 'Spinners'
'Bevan's Variety' *see G.
    macrorrhizum* 'Bevan's
    Variety'
bicknellii, 105
'Bill Wallis' *see G.
    pyrenaicum* 'Bill Wallis'
'Birch Double' *see G.
    himalayense* 'Plenum'
'Bittersweet' *see G.
    pratense* 'Bittersweet'
biuncinatum, 105
'Black Ice', 75
bohemicum, 105
'Brookside', 12, 32, 49,
    106, *106*, *144*
brutium, 72, 106
brycei, 145
'Buxton's Blue'/'Buxton's
    Variety' *see G.
    wallichianum* 'Buxton's
    Variety'
caffrum, 145
canariense, 83, 107
*candicans/candidum see
    G. lambertii* 'Swansdown'
× *cantabrigiense*, *51*, 107
    'Biokovo', 107
carolinianum, 107
cataractarum, *51*, 52, 107
'Cedric Morris', *see G.
    sanguineum* 'Cedric
    Morris'
'Chantilly', *48*, 50, 75
cinereum var. *cinereum*, 44,
    46, 107
    'Ballerina', 45, 108
    'Lawrence Flatman', 45,

45, 108, *108*
var. *obtusilobum*, 108
var. *subcaulescens*, 47,
    47, 108
var. *subcaulescens*
    'Giuseppii', 108
var. *subcaulescens*
    'Splendens', 108
'Claridge Druce' *see G. ×
    oxonianum* 'Claridge
    Druce'
clarkei, 108
    'Kashmir Pink', 12, *82*,
        109
    'Kashmir Purple', 31,
        48, 69, 71, 109
    'Kashmir White', 22,
        33, 109, *109*
collinum, 31, 49, *51*, 109
columbinum, 141
'Czakor' *see G.
    macrorrhizum* 'Czakor'
dahuricum, 50, 109
dalmaticum, 46, *46*, *51*,
    52, 109
    'Album', 46, 110
delavayi (of gardens) *see
    G. sinense*
    (true form), 70
'Dilys', 55, 76
dissectum, 142
donianum, 110
endressii, 20, *21*, 26, 32,
    33, 38, 49, 50, 54, 62, 110,
    110
    'Wargrave Pink', *32*, *110*
'Elsbeth' *see G.
    sanguineum* 'Elsbeth'
erianthum, 31, 52, 110
'Eric Clement' *see G. ×
    monacense* 'Eric
    Clement'
*eriostemon see G.
    platyanthum*
farreri, 47, 111
favosum, 111
fremontii, 111
'Galactic' *see G. pratense*
    'Galactic'
'Giuseppii' *see G.
    cinereum* var.
    subcaulescens 'Giuseppii'

156

Geranium (*continued*)
glaberrimum, 111
'Glenluce' *see G.*
   sanguineum 'Glenluce'
gracile, 67, 111
grandiflorum see G.
   himalayense
'Gravetye' *see G.*
   himalayense 'Gravetye'
grevilleanum see G.
   lambertii
gymnocaulon, 111
'Gypsy' *see G.* ×
   lindavicum 'Gypsy'
himalayense, 24, 26, 33,
   48, 49, 112, *144*
   'Gravetye,' 25, 28, 33,
      112, *112*
   'Irish Blue', 25, 112, *144*
   'Plenum', 33, *71*, *94*,
      113
'Holden' *see G.*
   sanguineum 'Holden'
'Hollywood' *see G.* ×
   oxonianum 'Hollywood'
ibericum ssp. *ibericum*,
   25, 32, 67, 113
incanum var. *multifidum*
   44, *60*, 145
incisum see G. nervosum
'Ingwersen's Variety' *see*
   G. macrorrhizum
   'Ingwersen's Variety'
'Irish Blue' *see G.*
   himalayense 'Irish Blue'
'Jenny Bloom' *see G.* ×
   lindavicum 'Apple
   Blossom'
'Joan Baker' *see G.*
   phaeum var. *lividum*
   'Joan Baker'
'Johnson's Blue', *11*, 12,
   24, 28, 32, *113*, 114
'Joy', *60*, 76, *76*
'Jubilee Pink' *see G.*
   sanguineum 'Jubilee
   Pink'
'Kashmir Blue',
   114
'Kashmir Pink/Purple/
   White' *see G. clarkei*
'Kate' 114
'Kate Folkard' *see G.*
   'Kate'
kerberi, 114
kishtvariense, 31, 68, 69,
   71, 114
krameri, 114
'Lady Moore' *see G.* ×
   oxonianum 'Lady Moore'
lambertii, *71*, 114
   'Swansdown', 115
lanuginosum, 115
'Lawrence Flatman' *see*
   G. cinereum 'Lawrence
   Flatman'

libani, 39, 52, 115, *115*
'Lily Lovell' *see G.*
   phaeum 'Lily Lovell'
× *lindavicum* 'Alanah',
   116
   'Apple Blossom', 46,
      47, 116
   'Gypsy', 116
   'Lissadell', 116, *116*
'Lissadell' *see G.* ×
   lindavicum 'Lissadell'
lividum see G. phaeum
   var. *lividum*
'Lohfelden' *see G.*
   macrorrhizum
   'Lohfelden'
lucidum, 142
macrorrhizum, 33, 36, 49,
   52, 54, 79, 84, 116
   'Album', *18*, 33, 36,
      48, 116
   'Bevan's Variety', 36,
      117, *117*
   'Czakor', 33, 117
   'Ingwersen's Variety',
      33, 36, 36, 117
   'Lohfelden', 117
   'Ridsko', 117
   Spessart', 33, 117
   'Variegatum', 41, *41*,
      48, 52, 117
macrostylum, 72, 117
maculatum, 26, 73, 87,
   118
   'Album', 20, 118
maderense, 40, 83, 118
× *magnificum*, *11*, 23, 25,
   32, *42*, *51*, 52, 118
'Majus' *see G. phaeum*
   var. *lividum* 'Majus'
malviflorum, 38, *39*, 52,
   72, 118
'Mary Mottram', 118
mascatense, 120
'Mavis Simpson' *see G.* ×
   riversleaianum 'Mavis
   Simpson'
'Max Frei' *see G.*
   sanguineum 'Max Frei'
'Mayflower' *see G.*
   sylvaticum 'Mayflower'
meeboldii see G.
   himalayense
'Minutum' *see G.*
   sanguineum 'Minutum'
molle, 142
× *monacense*, 49, 120, *120*
   nothovar *anglicum*,
      119, 120
   'Eric Clement', 120
   'Muldoon', 37, 50, 52,
      120
'Mrs Kendall Clark' *see*
   G. pratense 'Mrs
   Kendall Clark'

'Muldoon' *see G.* ×
   monacense 'Muldoon'
nepalense, 120
nervosum, 120, *121*
'Nimbus', *28*, 29, *48*,
   122, *144*
nodosum, 37, *48*, 52, 62,
   122, *122*
'Nora Bremner', 76
ocellatum, 122
oreganum, 31, 86, 122
orientalitibeticum, 50, 123
× *oxonianum*, 26, 33, 49,
   123
   'A.T. Johnson', 65, 123
   'Claridge Druce', 37,
      52, 123
   'Hollywood', 123
   'Lady Moore', 19, 123,
      123
   'Rose Clair', *55*, 123
   'Sherwood', 123
   'Southcombe Double',
      124
   'Southcombe Star', 124
   'Thurstonianum', 19,
      31, *84*, 124
   'Walter's Gift', 50, *51*,
      124, *124*
   'Winscombe', 32, 124
'Pagoda', 76
palmatum, 83, 124
palustre, 47, 55, 73, 124
papuanum, 125
'Patricia', 77, *144*
peloponnesiacum, *52*, *72*,
   125
phaeum, 36, 37, 49, 55,
   57, 62, 125
   'Album', 37, 125
   'Lily Lovell', 12, 28,
      32, 55, 125, *126*
   var. *lividum*, 125
   var. *lividum* 'Joan
      Baker', 72, 125
   var. *lividum* 'Majus',
      125
   'Samobor', *60*, 126
   'Taff's Jester', 126
   'Variegatum', 37, 40,
      48, 126
'Philippe Vapelle', *48*,
   50, 77, *77*, *144*
platyanthum, 52, 126
platypetalum, 25, 32, 67,
   126, *126*
pogonanthum, *51*, 126
polyanthes, 126
potentilloides, 127
pratense, 28, 32, 47, 49,
   50, 54, 55, 62, 127, *128*,
   142
   forma *albiflorum*, 20,
      33, *60*, 127
   'Bicolor' *see G. pratense*

   'Striatum'
   'Bittersweet', 32, 128
pratense 'Galactic', 128
   'Mrs Kendall Clark',
      25, 25–6, 32, 128
   'Plenum Album', 19,
      129
   'Plenum Caeruleum',
      22, 24, *71*, 129, *142*
   'Plenum Violaceum'
      24, *71*, 129
   'Purpureum Plenum'
      see G. pratense
      'Plenum Violaceum'
   'Silver Queen', 22,
      128
   'Striatum', 25, 26, 128,
      129
'Prince Regent' *see G.*
   asphodeloides 'Prince
   Regent'
procurrens, 29–30, 40,
   129, *130*
pseudosibiricum, 130
psilostemon, *11*, 14–16,
   15, 16, 49, 52, 130
   'Bressingham Flair', 14,
      66, 130
pulchrum, 51, 145
punctatum see G. ×
   monacense
purpureum, 142
purpusii see G.
   schiedeanum
pusillum, 143
pylzowianum, 70, 130
pyrenaicum, 52, 84, 131,
   131, 143
   forma *albiflorum*, 72,
      131
   'Bill Wallis', 131
   'Rebecca', 77
rectum 131
   album *see G. clarkei*
   'Kashmir White'
reflexum, 131
refractum, 131
renardii, 20, 31, *48*, 50,
   132, *132*
   'Whiteknights', 31, 79,
      132
richardsonii, 132
'Ridsko' *see G.*
   macrorrhizum 'Ridsko'
riversleaianum 132
   'Mavis Simpson', 33,
      39–40, *55*, *90*, 132
   'Russell Prichard', *17*,
      39–40, *40*, *132*, 133
rivulare, 133
robertianum, 63, 133, 143
robustum, *48*, 52, *71*, 146
'Rose Clair' *see G.* ×
   oxonianum 'Rose Clair'
rotundifolium, 143

Geranium (*continued*)

rubescens, 133
rubifolium, *51*, 133
rupretchii, 133
'Russell Prichard' *see G. riversleaianum* 'Russell Prichard'
'Salome', 29–30, *71*, 133
'Samobor' *see G. phaeum* 'Samobor'
sanguineum, *2*, 49, 52, 62, 67, 134, *134*, 143
　'Album', *27*, 28, 33, 134, *135*
　'Alan Bloom', 134
　'Cedric Morris' *51*, *55*, 134, *135*
　'Elsbeth', 134
　'Glenluce', 31, 134
　'Holden', 134
　'Jubilee Pink', 31, *55*, 134
　lancastriense see G. sanguineum var. *striatum*
　'Max Frei', 52, *55*, 134
　'Minutum', 134
　'Nanum' *see G. sanguineum* 'Minutum'
　'Prostratum' *see G. sanguineum* 'Minutum'
　'Shepherds Warning', 31, 134
　var. *striatum*, 28, 30, *30*, 33, *55*, 134
schideanum, 136
'Sea Fire', 77
'Sea Pink', 77
'Sea Spray', 77
sessiliflorum ssp. *novaezelandiae*, *51*, 136
　ssp. *novaezelandiae* 'Nigricans', 45, 136
'Shepherd's Warning' *see G. sanguineum* 'Shepherds Warning'
'Sherwood' *see G. × oxonianum* 'Sherwood'
shikokianum, 136
sibiricum, 136
'Silver Queen' *see G. pratense* 'Silver Queen'
sinense, 60, 136
soboliferum, 136
'Southcombe Double/

'Southcombe Star' *see G. × oxonianum*
'Spessart' *see G. macrorrhizum* 'Spessart'
'Spinners', 32, *34*, 49, 137, *137*, *144*
'Splendens' *see G. cinereum* var. *subcaulescens* 'Splendens'
'Stanhoe', 138
stapfianum, 138
　roseum see G. orientalibeticum
'Starlight' *see G. asphodeloides* 'Starlight'
strigosum see G. nervosum
subulato-stipulatum, 138
'Swansdown' *see G. lambertii* 'Swansdown'
swatense, 138
'Syabru' *see G. wallichianum* 'Syabru'
sylvaticum, 47, 138, 143
　forma *albiflorum*, 138
　'Album', *18*, 20, 49, 138
　'Amy Doncaster', 138
　'Baker's Pink', *72*, *72*, 138
　'Mayflower', 49, 139, *139*
sylvaticum ssp. *pseudosibiricum see G. pseudosibiricum*
　ssp. *rivulare see G. rivulare*
　forma *roseum*, 139
　var. *wanneri*. 139
　'Wengen' *see G. sylvaticum* 'Baker's Pink'
'Taff's Jester' *see G. phaeum* 'Taff's Jester'
thunbergii, 139
'Thurstonianum' *see G. × oxonianum* 'Thurstonianum'
transbaicalicum, 139
traversii var. *elegans*, 39, 60, 139
trilophum, 139
tuberosum, 39, 140
versicolor, 38, 49, 62, 140
viscosissimum, 140
wallichianum, 140

'Buxton's Variety', 28–9, *51*, 52, 54, 65, 140, *140*
'Syabru', 7, 140
'Walter's Gift' *see G. × oxonianum* 'Walter's Gift'
wanneri see G. sylvaticum var. *wanneri*
'Wargrave Pink' *see G. endressii* 'Wargrave Pink'
'Whiteknights' *see G. renardii* 'Whiteknights'
'Winscombe' *see G. × oxonianum* 'Winscombe'
wlassovianum, 31–2, *51*, 52, *88*, 141
yesoense, 141
yunnanense, 69, 141
Gerard, John, 62
Grigson, Geoffrey, 63
Grout, Joan and Robin, 118

Hardy Plant Society, 10
Hedgerow Cranesbill *see G. pyrenaicum*
Herb Robert *see G. robertianum*
Hibberd, David, 74, 105
Hobson, John, 79

Ingwersen, Walter, 25, 31, 64, 115, 116

Johnson, A.T., 38, 64, 114, 123, 134
Johnson, Hugh, 10
Jones, Joy, 12, 93

Knechtel, Elke and Ken, 88

Lancaster, Roy, 66, 67–70, 114
Langthorns Plantery, 123
Lee, Rosemary, 82
Lesser Herb Robert *see G. purpureum*
Lindsay, Nancy, 6
Linnaeus (Carl von Linné), 8
Little Robin *see G. purpureum*
Long Stalked Cranesbill *see G. columbinum*

Martin, Rev Keble, 85

Meadow Cranesbill *see G. pratense*
Moore, Lady, 19
Mountain Cranesbill *see G. pyrenaicum*

Norton, Andrew, 85
Nottle, Trevor, 92–9

Parer, Robin, 89
Parkinson, John, 62
Planting ideas *see* Associations
Pests and Diseases, 54, 56
Propagation, 57–61
　Cuttings, 57
　Division, 57
　Geranium cinereum etc, 59
　Root Cuttings, 57–8
　Seed, 58–9
Pyrenean Cranesbill *see G. pyrenaicum*

RHS Wisley Trial, 25
Robinson, William, 64
Rohde, Eleanour Sinclair, 143
Roller, Carol, 89
Round-leaved Cranesbill *see G. rotundifolium*

Sackville-West, Vita, 19
Savill Garden, 44–5
Shearer, Malcolm, 100–101
Shining Cranesbill *see G. lucidum*
Sissinghurst Castle, 19
Small-flowered Cranesbill *see G. pusillum*
Southcombe Nursery, 124
Strangman, Elizabeth, 126, 133

Taffler, Stephen, 126
Thomas, Graham Stuart, 25, 66, 112
Thompson, Dennis, 86, 89, 122

Washfield Nursery, 126
Whittlesey, John, 89
Wood Cranesbill *see G. sylvaticum*

Yeo, Peter, 66, 69, 73, 78, 110, 116, 123